AFRICAN SPIRITUALITY: ON BECOMING ANCESTORS

Anthony Ephirim-Donkor

Africa World Press, Inc.

P.O. Box 1892
Trenton, NJ 08607

P.O. Box 48
Asmara, ERITREA

Africa World Press, Inc.

P.O. Box 1892
Trenton, NJ 08607

P.O. Box 48
Asmara, ERITREA

First Printing 1997
Second Printing April 1998

Book design: Jonathan Gullery
Cover design: Aaron J. Wilson

Library of Congress Cataloging-in Publication Data

Ephirim-Donkor, Anthony.
    African spirituality : on becoming ancestors / Anthony Ephirim
-Donkor.
       p. cm.
    Includes bibliographical references and index.
    ISBN 0-86543-552-9. -- ISBN 0-86543-553-7 (alk. paper)
      1. Akan (African people)–Religion. 2. Ancestor worship.
    3. Ghana–Religion. 4. Africa, Sub-Saharan--Religion. I. Title.
BL2480.A4E64 1997
299'.683385–dc21   97-3148
                                          CIP

CONTENTS

PART I

THE PERSONALITY

PART II

CHILDHOOD

PART III

ADULTHOOD

To Comfort Efua Tawiah (Wallace) Donkor

ACKNOWLEDGEMENTS

I take this opportunity to express my heartfelt thanks and appreciation to my mentor, friend, and advisor, Dr. James Fowler of Emory University. It was Dr. Fowler's theory of faith and moral development that led me to my cultural reclamation and the writing of this book.

I am grateful to Michael Harrison for his fruitful discussions on some ideas and concepts of the Akan people in relation to Western hermeneutical thoughts. Special thanks to Sarah and Professor Herron, and Julia and Joseph Bundy, for their initial and ongoing support for me and being parents to me and my family. And to the members of Suwanee Parish United Methodist Church: I thank you for the love you showed towards me, my wife, and our children.

To my mother, Amma Emissah, and my sister, Efua Akon, I thank you with all my heart for being there for me. Finally, my whole-hearted thanks to my life's partner and wife, Comfort; our children, Anthony and Julia and Kow Awona. I love you.

PREFACE

I would begin my discussions or teaching by saying or writing "Africa" on the board and then ask my students to say or write anything that came to mind upon hearing or seeing the word Africa. Words like superstition, voodoo, tribe, jungle, village, animals, ancestral worship, pagan, hunger, poverty, huts, rites, witchery, and many more would always come up. But by end of session—or of semester—the students would have come to some understanding of the universality of such terms. For one thing, most of what we are taught about others is in one way or another informed by our contextual prejudices. People make judgement about others without the slightest inkling that, perhaps, they too may be partakers of the same or similar realities.

A recurring point of discussion in relation to Black spirituality is the so-called "worship of the dead" among Africans. But don't all peoples "worship,"—i.e., venerate or show reverence for—the dead? I know of soldiers on every continent who visit war memorials and wail, and whole countries that set aside national (memorial) days to remember their dead. I have seen many people visit crematories and leave flowers on the graves of their loved ones, and have observed many presidents and heads of state lay wreaths at the tombs of unknown (dead) soldiers or national heros.

The fact is that in Africa deliberate efforts are made to "worship" the dead regularly. The reason is that the dead do not really die but continue to live forever as ancestors. And that is what this book is about—how the Akan people become ancestors.

In general, the book is aimed at three audiences. First, Africanists, cultural anthropologists, and sociologists will find this book indispensable. It deals with every facet of Akan culture from the perspective of an insider who now stands outside looking in critically. From metaphysics and religion, existential issues and socio-political organization, to rites delineating the stages of human development, it brings the Akan ritual life in its totality into focus.

Secondly, the book is addressed to psychologists and students of developmental and psychosocial psychology. It may be used as a resource for African developmental studies by looking at models extant among the Akan people. It may also be used in dialogue with Western psychological scholarship in the search for a cross-cultural interpretive framework.

Finally, it is addressed to African Americans in general. In recent decades the African American community has undergone a series of identity shifts in its quest for a cross-cultural heritage and renaissance. I base this claim on my own experience as a pastor who has taught Black spirituality and cultural reclamation to his African American congregation.

As a former pastor of three small African American congregations at Suwanee, Georgia, that later merged under my leadership into Suwanee Parish United Methodist Church, I know the yearning of the laity to reclaim some aspects of the lost heritage. I was attempting to educate them, but in the process I too came to be educated. As an African I came to understand the anguish and experiences of my African American brothers and sisters across the Atlantic. And now that I am no longer a pastor, but a representative of the Akan culture, I continue in another capacity the discussions I began at Suwanee with some members of the church.

For one thing I was quite anxious. Yes, I was Black, but I was also an African. However, I took the pastorate as a challenge, for after all, one of my strengths was in cross-cultural faith development. But I discovered something unique, or should I say, together we discovered a shared propinquity. This was manifested in resounding "yes" responses. I don't mean the call-and-response trademark of Black worship, though even that had a meaningful resolve to it, perhaps for the first time. By that I mean knowing about the contextual origins of the call and response between the king, on the one hand, and his or her orators and citizens, on the other. In the absence of the king or the elder in the Black diaspora, the pastor or minister assumed the roles of the king, elder, and priest by continuing the call-and-response carryover from Africa in the context of the Black church. (*Infra*, pp. 166-168)

But what I am referring to in relation to the "yes" responses, like the call and response, is my ability to offer an African hermeneutical approach to the lost African American heritage. When one understands *why* a person does the things one does, it is quite exhilarating and often emits responses like "uh-huh." That is, finding an anchor for some of the innate depositions a people have. While this book by no means addresses all aspects of the African cultural heritage, it is a start.

Furthermore, this book stems from my own attempts to come to an understanding of myself cross-culturally in the United States of America. After taking a number of psychology courses in theological seminary during which I was asked to construct my life's tapestry, I realized that I was a communal being, defined and shaped in the ethos of the Akan. This led me to appreciate my own culture for the first time. That is, standing outside my own culture, I realized how different I was racially and culturally. These differences led me to critically reflect upon my life. But rather than conceive of these differences as weaknesses, they became my strength and uniqueness, thus my cultural reclamation.

Anthony Ephirim-Donkor

PART I
THE
PERSONALITY

Chapter 1

INTRODUCTION

The Akan people are found in the modern countries of Ghana and the Ivory Coast. This study focuses on those in Ghana, approximately half of Ghana's population, and uses them as a resource to examine the overall Akan conception of human development. This is the first study of its kind that looks at African developmental processes. It uses rites of initiation in the context of transformation during the maturational processes, i.e., how these rites influence the individual socio-politically, psychologically, economically, and spiritually.

The Akan people are bound together by a common religion and belief in *Nana Nyame* (God), language,[1] politics and ethos. The name *Akan* itself is illustrative, for it has to do with beginnings. Its etymology, I discovered, has several renditions. *Kan* has been interpreted as: first, to lead, foremost, genuine, pure, light, bright, intentionality, to count or reckon, to read, and to cry or wail as during the dirges sung at funerals. Some of my discussants maintain that the Akan people were the first people to walk the earth. Others contend they were the first to be endowed with the art of oratory, the speech-makers of public forums. This would be consistent with the view that the Akan people were the first to have seen light and would therefore, as leaders, have a message to impart to others. One thing on which they concur was that the Akan people were the first or leaders (*akanfo*) in whatever they were in the light of *kan*. All of these meanings of *kan*, as will be shown in this study, are related to the central understanding of existence. This conception has several phases.

From their beliefs in reincarnation, conception, birth, education, ethical existence and generativity, eldership, death, and ancestorhood, there are culturally defined rites marking individual phases of development, delineating *obra bo* [2] (ethical existence and generativity). The individual must live an ideal ethic (*obra pa*) in the corporeal world, leading to the conferral of the title elder (*Nana*). In the ancestral world called *Samanadze*, the elders automatically attain ancestorhood, joining the immortal community of ancestors called *Nananom Nsamanfo*. This model is predicated on a theory of the personality that has its ontological basis in God (*Nana Nyame*), and the archetypal woman and her children who constituted the ideal *ebusua* or matrikin.

The ideal life itself is predicated upon the God-given existential purpose called *nkrabea*. The elusiveness of the purpose of being, however, makes life quite precarious. Ethical life therefore is concerned with knowing the precise nature of the individual's purpose of being, the discovery of which may lead to the ideal existence. The inevitability of death, however, means that the ideal life, the attainment of eldership or perfection, and ancestorhood may not be realized. Yet death is the means by which one can achieve immortality. When the individual dies without fulfilling his or her purpose of being, the deceased is reincarnated as many times as necessary in order to fulfill the God-given purpose of being. But the fulfillment of it does not necessarily lead to eldership because ethical existence and generativity must be construed socially as the ideal. In the final analysis, only the *ebusua*, the matrix and custodian of ethical existence and generativity, confers eldership.

My research method is participatory observation of ritual processes. By that I mean the process by which the individual's (participant's) subjective experiences are critically assessed by the community (observers) of faith in order to ensure the veracity of those experiences. Thereupon the appropriate maturational stage title is conferred on the individual. To the Akan people, this method of objectifying ritual stages is a normative process handed down from antiquity to contemporary generations.

The lingering nature of ethical existence and generativity means that living must be acted out existentially to ensure the ideal life. The ideal is measured in terms of altruism, invariably construed as having found one's existential purpose of being.

Although ethical existence and generativity is thought of as an individual quest, it is incumbent upon the community to safeguard its content. Disorder engendered by unethical life has broader existential and metaphysical repercussions, threatening the homeostatic relationship between the mundane and the ancestral worlds. In order to maintain cosmic balance, annual, seasonal, forty-day-cyclical festivals and situational rites are performed. These rites call for communal participation. Even absentee citizens are represented by other family members or their lineage heads. Led by the king and his or her elders, society is brought to existential-divine harmony through propitiatory worship.

When I was growing up, I participated in some of these communal rites as well as private rites of initiation, such as twins, purification, and divination. Now as an adult I have revisited, observed, and when possible participated in some of the same rites. Some of the rites, like funerals and festivals, could not be enacted summarily, so I have made several trips to Ghana in order to participate in or observe the rites in progress.

Rites have their own parameters. That is, there are those exclusively meant for girls and women, those for boys and men, and others inclusive of all ages and sexes. To gather information on these differences, I consulted teachers, nurses and midwives (both traditional and Western-trained), farmers, fishermen and fishmongers, children, elders, and kings. I was also able to convene discussion groups on various aspects of the Akan culture. These for the most part were recorded and analyzed with the help of my assistants. We had randomly discussed specific issues aimed at obtaining conventional viewpoints as opposed to traditional dogma.

From 1986 to 1993, I made several visits to Ghana and Liberia, during which, from 1979 to 1982, I lived in the town of Gbarnga. In Ghana I was based at Winneba, a town of over 60,000 people, and Gomoa Mprumem, a farming town of 5,000 citizens. Most of the research was carried out in the Gomoa and the Awutu-Effutu-Senya districts. In the latter district, my assistants and I talked with representatives from the Asante, the Akuapim, the Khawu, and the Nzema who reside there. In general, our research is reflective of the Akan culture.

This structural model utilizes myths and concepts, rites, dreams, and symbolic elements that form the basis for human development among the Akan people. The interpretive framework in this study has been influenced by Erik Erikson[3] and James Fowler.[4] They are known for their work on the ego and psychosocial stages of the life cycle and constructive developmental research in faith and moral development. Fowler has also studied the cognitive patterns of knowing, valuing, interpreting, and reasoning that constitute the basis for moral and ethical understanding. They are used within the socio-political, psychological, anthropological, and spiritual context of the Akan people.

We should not assume that age is always the determining factor with regard to rituals marking maturation or passage to a new status. I discovered that there are sociological designations that are based solely on exceptional abilities and dexterity. Individuals who fall under this classification must nonetheless conform to certain rules and norms of behavior associated with their stage. If, for instance, a person fails to exhibit the appropriate norms of behavior and cognition, then society refers to such an individual as *onyimpa gyangyan* (useless person) or *kwasiampanyin* (stupid person).

Areas of our research include the conceptual theory of personality; reincarnation, conception, birth, post-partum care, and early childhood; orality and the cognitive operational patterns of knowing and reasoning; meaning making and patterns of interpreting existence and generativity; eldership; and death and ancestorhood.

First, we studied the patterns of ritual development and generativity. We examined the rites that are commensurate with the maturational stages and the role the matrikin plays in performing these rites. Beginning with reincarnation, we studied conception, birth, intrapartal and post-partum, and neonatal care.

Second, we examined the pedagogical apparatus of cognitive development and the epigenetic basis for orality. Since orality is the foundation for social, economic, political, and spiritual life, our aim was to discover those operational patterns of orality. Studying children between the ages of six through fourteen, we had them perform various tasks. We questioned children who sold various ingredients. Different combinations of items were bought at varying prices. Then we offered them money in large bills to see how they went about computing the transaction and determining the right change due us. Furthermore, we wanted to ascertain how much children committed to memory and their ability to add or subtract.[5] Finally, we wanted to know the effect of Western influence on children in shaping their world view, that is, whether or not the Western emphasis on writing affected orality one way or another. This was achieved artistically by asking school children to draw or paint anything of interest to them.

Finally, attention was given to adulthood or what the Akan people call *obra bo* (ethical existence and generativity). Adulthood begins when the individual is morally and ethically concerned with existential issues. In general, marriage and employment mark the beginning of adulthood. This is when the individual is able to distance himself or herself from significant others, engage in critical reflection, and make moral and ethical decisions.

To make ethical choices is to engage in critical reflection, especially during late adulthood. Critical reflection and an ideal life usher the individual into eldership. The attainment of eldership means that the elder must be in the state of perfection based on the collective infallibility of the elders. They are concerned with maintaining existential and metaphysical order, often in the face of hostility by the young. Upon his or her death, the elder becomes an ancestor of perpetual remembrance.

My aim is to develop a developmental model based on the Akan people, one which will serve as the basis for a better view of African life. This way of conceptualizing the Akan people is not new, but this is the first study of its kind that examines the Akan people from a developmental perspective related to Western psychosocial and constructive developmental theories.

This endeavor stems from my attempt to come to a cross-cultural understanding of myself. After taking a number of developmental courses in theological seminary, I began to take a critical look at myself relationally and culturally. I discovered and came to the appreciation that I am a communal being, nurtured and shaped by the ethos of the Akan people. This study discloses the way I perceive myself relationally; it defines and forms my moral and ethical responsibility.

I have divided this study into three parts. Part I must be read and understood as a metaphysical drama. It begins with the theoretical perspectives of the personality as seen by ethnographers. In general, the reviewed literature and findings deal with only few elements, and then only within the confines of previous studies. Even where new concepts are examined, they are not discussed in relation to the overall conception of the Akan world view. This is precisely why a comprehensive exploration of the personality is needed.

In chapter three I begin with the Akan cosmology as a way of offering the ontological basis for all theological, anthropological, sociopolitical, philosophical, and spiritual speculations. Then the concept of community is discussed in relation to the mother's blood as the basis for the physicality of the individual.

The individual is not only a physical being, but a spiritual and a divine individual as well. Thus, the paternal (spiritual) and the Godly (divine) attributes of the individual are explored. Eighteen spiritual and divine essences and their manifestations are studied. They are also shown, together with the mother's blood, to coalesce into a holistic personality.

Part II focusses on childhood. Until the beginning of consciousness or awareness, children are thought to have paranormal capabilities that enable them to maintain close rapport with their spiritual siblings and mother. But with awareness comes the task of educating children into full adults. From simple rituals to sophisticated tasks designed to inculcate both cognitive development and moral and ethical responsibility, adults equip children to become good citizens during the educational stage of their development.

Part III looks at adulthood——the period of ethical existence and generativity, a time when the individual is existentially responsible for his or her own actions. Paradoxically, adulthood is a period of independence from significant others as one enters into new relationships; but at the same time the adult is dependent on the matrikin folks, the matrix of meaning-making.

The generative individual is the person who leads an ideal, altruistic life, the prerequisite to eldership. In recognition of the individual's altruism, one's matrikin folk confers on him or her the highest existential title, Elder. After having mastered and integrated the act of living, the elder is in the position to bequeath to contemporary generations acts of ideal living. As repositories of sacred traditions, the elders are bound by a higher moral imperative— accountability to their eternal predecessors, the ancestors. Standing on the threshold of ancestorhood themselves, the elders have already transcended death and look forward to living face-to-face with their eternal counterparts.

However, death is not a welcoming phenomenon, even though it is the means by which the elder ultimately becomes an ancestor. When death occurs the corpse is ritually prepared and given a fitting burial. After forty days, the spiritual personality (*Osaman*) of the deceased departs the physical world and returns to the world of the ancestors. There the spiritual personality is put on trial and, if found worthy, admitted into the company of the ancestors. However, if the spiritual personality is found to have led an unethical life on earth, then it is pronounced guilty and excluded from ancestorhood. The guilty spiritual personality may have to reincarnate to undo its evils. The ancestors, however, watch over the affairs of the world from their vantage abode of heaven (*Samanadze*).

Notes

1. J. G. Christaller, *Dictionary of the Asante and Fante Language Called Tshi (Twi)*, 2d. ed. (Basel Evangelical Misson Society, 1933), xiii-xvi.
2. My usage of Akan terms and concepts are in the Mfantse language.
3. See Erik Erikson, *A Way of Looking at Things: Selected Papers From 1930 to 1980* (New York: Wm. Morton & co., 1987).
4. See James Fowler, *Stages of Faith: The Psychology of Human Development and the Quest for Meaning* (New York: Harper & Row, 1981).
5. J. Piaget, *Six Psychological Studies* (New York: Vantage Books, 1967), 49.

Chapter 2

CONCEPTUAL
THEORIES

....

Sankofa is an Akan courtly word which means to return and retrieve. I have heard it applied to unrepentant individuals during adjudication to urge them to own up to their wrongdoing: that is, there is nothing wrong in saying one is wrong. In this way the individual's sentence is reduced considerably. Again, during deliberations an elder may err in protocol and when reminded of it would quickly correct himself in order to avoid paying a penalty. From the socio-historical and political standpoint, it is incumbent on the elders to correct or undo a past injustice within the context of *sankofa*. The point is, it's perfectly legal for the elders—in fact, it is their moral and civic duty—to review the past in the hopes of ameliorating the present and the future.

And as an Akan *elder* myself, I undertake to examine the metaphysical past of the Akan peoples that has given rise to conventional spiritual speculations. This is necessary because an optimistic future is meaningless without both the past and present. Thus, I am interested in the contributions made by ethnographers who have grappled with the Akan conceptual theory of the personality.

What is known by the Akan people themselves has been pre-
served as oral tradition and handed down from antiquity by the elders
as ancient sayings (*abakwasem* or *tsetsensem*) or sayings of the elders
(*mpanyinsem*) to succeeding generations. In addition to these oral histories there are written sources bequeathed to us by the early Europeans
which, for the most part, corroborate the ancient sayings concerning
the spiritual basis of personality.

One of the earliest sources we have is by Pieter de Marees,[1] a
young Dutchman who wrote in the early 1600s. He described the
Akan people as, among other things, having "fine stature" and "well
chiselled bodies," as being "as strong as trees," and as "...surpass[ing]
all other Moors of Africa in body and stature, so that the Men of this
area may be considered the strongest and most handsome (both in
their character and strength) in the whole country [=continent]." [2]

Perhaps unbeknownst to de Marees, these same descriptions figure prominently in Akan thought. His notion of beauty and use of the
tree metaphor, for example, are consistent with Akan aestheticism, as
we will see below. The elders often display strong nostalgic feelings
about the predecessors of the present-day Akan people. They believe
their ancestors were much stronger, taller, and more beautiful. But
their concern was spiritual, too: they maintain that people nowadays
are oblivious to the rites and ethos that are necessary for ensuring metaphysical and existential balance. One could easily be tempted to blame
the elders for this state of affairs, but I am reminded rather of their inde-
fatigable effort to educate and pass on the traditions entrusted to them
to succeeding generations. The blame, they point out, lies with the present generation's characterization of the past as antiquated.

While de Marees offers valuable information about the physical
characteristics of the Akan people, the nineteenth-century Europeans
also began delving into the metaphysical and religious thought of the
Akan people. In the late nineteenth century, A. B. Ellis[3] offered some
thoughts on three personality concepts and their manifestations, namely, the *kra*, the *sunsum*, and the *srahman*. To Ellis the guarding spirit of
the human being is call *kra*, which he maintains "ordinarily dwells in
a living man." As a spirit that protects, it must be propitiated to ensure
its continued protection. The *kra*, Ellis contends, is generally interpreted as soul, but he dismisses any attempt to compare the Akan con-

ception of the *kra* with the European concept of the soul.[4] To Ellis the European conception of the soul is that it departs the body during death, but the same cannot be said about the *kra*, he argues. He believes that the *kra* upon the death of a person changes into a shadowy form called *sisa* in the after-life. The *sisa* awaits reincarnation into *kra* at the deceased's house. However, after an unspecified time of failure to reincarnate, the *sisa* relocates to a country "beyond the River Volta."

The *kra* also plays a crucial role in the dream-world. According to Ellis, when one sleeps the *kra* leaves the body temporarily in pursuit of the dream-world adventures. Quite often, the temporary departure of the *kra* creates opportunities for malignant shadowy forms to invade the body, thereby causing illness to the person when he or she awakes from sleep. For this reason both the *kra* and *sisa* are propitiated to induce the *sisa's* benignity and restoration of wholeness to the *kra*.

Ellis defines the *sunsum* as "spirit", though it also means "shadow." In the form of a ghost (*srahman*), the *sunsum* of the deceased continues to live forever in the ancestral world, called *Srahmanadze*, believed to be underground.[5] At Srahmanadze the ghosts are called *Asrahmanfo*, the spirits of the departed ones who watch over the state.

From the standpoint of Ellis, the personality has the *kra* which has existence of its own, and the *sunsum* or spirit which become a ghost or *srahman* at death. The ghostly form makes its residence in the ancestral world, exhibiting the same characteristics as the defunct person, but now overseeing the living from the vantage point of Srahmanadze.

The question is: Why didn't Ellis put the *kra* on the same footing with his European conception of the soul? Perhaps the way the concept was explained to him sounded different from his European understanding of the soul. But the fact that he tried to compare the two entities meant the he understood the function of the *kra* to be the same as or even superior to the European conception of the soul. Unwilling to accept that, he subordinated the *kra* to the European soul, a practice quite common throughout colonial Africa and meant to maintain Western hegemony.

Perhaps the single most in-depth study of any Akan sub-group was carried out by R. S. Rattray [6] in the 1920s. During his monumental study of the Asante people, at a time when their culture was impervious to foreigners, Rattray was able to gain the confidence of the aristocracy. This relationship led to some insightful discussions on the personality.

Concerning life's formative processes, Rattray posits that life begins when the *ntoro* (spirit) of the man mingles with the *mogya* (blood) of the woman to form the physical component of the personality.[7] To Rattray the *ntoro* and semen are the same, so that at birth a person is endowed with the masculine spirit and the feminine blood. Moreover, the *ntoro* is synonymous with the *sunsum*, "that spiritual element in a man or woman upon which depends...that force, personal magnetism, character, personality, power, soul,...health, wealth, worldly power, success in any venture, in fact everything that makes life at all worth living."[8] The *sunsum-ntoro* aspect of the person furthermore manifests itself in the form of fraternal cultic order connected with rivers or bodies of water and certain dietary prohibitions. The *sunsum-ntoro* component is endowed with immortality and protects group members while awaiting reincarnation. For Rattray, it is the *sunsum* (and not the *kra*, as Ellis maintains), that departs the body during the dream state to meet other spirits. The *sunsum-ntoro* can be lightweight or heavy, weak or strong, and good or evil. Consequently, it can be vulnerable during its nocturnal dream escapades.

The other concept Rattray discusses is the *kra*. He renders *kra* as "soul," having pre-existence of its own, although it may be the soul of a deceased ancestor. The *kra* is the life of a person, therefore its departure from the body is tantamount to death. Rattray also believes that the *kra* is appeased or "washed" on the day of the week it is believed to have come into existence.

He defines the *saman* as "ghost, an apparition, a spectre," which applies only to the dead in the land of ghosts (*samanfo*). However, the *saman* is not ethereal, since it retains its tangible form in the spirit world awaiting reincarnation into the same blood family. It has separate existence apart from the *kra* and the *ntoro-sunsum*.

Like the *saman*, the *sasa* is the "invisible spiritual power of a person or animal, which disturbs the mind of the living, or works a spell or mischief upon them, so that they suffer in various ways." The *sasa* is generally conceived as an evil spirit seeking revenge, and must be propitiated.

What Ellis's *sunsum-sisa* and Rattray's *sunsum-ntoro* have in common is that they are both endowed with the ability to reincarnate. However, for Rattray the *kra* does not change into *sisa* as Ellis contends because the *kra*, which Rattray has no problem defining as soul, has pre-existence of its own, making it impossible for any such transformation to take place. Rattray also believes that the *saman* has the ability to reincarnate.

Working on the behalf of the Gold Coast Government in the late 1940s on matters ranging from "native system of state finance" to "allegiance and jurisdiction," M. J. Field [9] touched on the personality concept. To Field, the human personality is composed of two entities, namely, the sunsum and the *kra*.[10] Field's conception of the *sunsum* is dualistic in nature, that is, one "Good and the other bad." The disposition and temperament of a person determines which "twin" is in control of the individual. The *sunsum*, moreover, departs the body during sleep or during the dream state.

During her ethnopsychiatric study,[11] Field discovered that the *sunsum* is the masculine, unifying, and protective component of every family unit. She observed that quite often divorces or potential problems in marriages are deferred or settled for the sake of the young. She observes:

> One ailing child whose parents were on bad terms and whose father was seldom at home was pronounced by the priest to be 'getting no *sunsum* from its father.' I was surprised, at my weekly clinic at Mframaso, to see how often it was the fathers and not mothers who brought children for treatment. The small child regards its father as its natural worshipper.[12]

She continues:

> When a sick child is brought to the Shrine the priest invariably seeks first for strife between the parents, a circumstance in which, it is held, no young child can thrive. One mother came spontaneously confessing that she had been planning to divorce her husband without due cause and therefore, she said, her child had fallen sick. The father of a sick child came admitting many offences against his family.
>
> Though the commonest reason assigned to sickness of a child is open quarrelling between parents, a number of mothers were blamed for adultery, refusal of intercourse with the father, and plain neglect of child. Several times a mother was told that her child was grieving for the father whom the mother left.[13]

Field defines the *kra* as the "spirit which makes the difference between a dead body and a living body." The *kra* is the animator or life-force of an otherwise inanimate body. The *kra*, she posits, is "an invisible double" and the essence of life; consequently it cannot leave the body "without causing sickness and death." The *kra* originates with the father while the body and blood have their source with the mother. And, because the *kra* is supplied by the father, a child and its father have the same *kra* and participate in the ceremonial paternal rituals. Field uses ntoro and *kra* interchangeably, but—most important-ly—she avers that the *kra* is not a phenomenon uniquely human; rather, animals and "germinating eggs" also have invisible doubles.

Field, like Rattray, posits that it is the *sunsum* that pervades the dream world, but she differs with Rattray on the provenance of the *kra*. To Field, the *kra* has its provenance with the father, consequently both father and child participate in the same paternal ritual ablution. Rattray, however, ascribes this paternal ritual ablution to the *sunsum-ntoro* phenomenon, while Field sees it as a *kra-ntoro* phenomenon. They both concur, however, that the blood of the mother forms the body.

James B. Christensen,[14] writing in the 1950s, attempts to ascertain whether the Mfantse (Fanti) sub-group belong to a dual or a single linear descent system. But in affirming the matrilineal system of descent among the Mfantse people, Christensen also points out that the emphasis placed by the Mfantse people on patrifiliation through what he calls *egyabosom* or "father's deity" suggests that they adhere to a system of double descent. However, Christensen's conceptual understanding of the personality is such that the woman is left with no physical or even blood ties to her child.

According to Christensen, the *kra*, the *sunsum (egyabosom)*, and the *bogya* or *mogya* (blood) all derive their source from the father. The *kra* or life-force (soul) of a person takes the form of blood and is transmitted by the father to his children. Moreover, at death the *kra* transforms itself into *saman* and journeys to Samanadze (ancestral world) to join the company of *Nsamanfo* (ancestors). In fact, Christensen insists that the Mfantse matrilineal—*ebusua* or blood—system of descent "is not composed of kinsmen related by blood" at all. He is of the opinion that the woman's blood is "weak" and therefore cannot be passed on to her children.

Concerning the *sunsum*, Christensen considers it to be another name for the *kra*, "contending that the *Kra* and *sunsum* are but different names for the soul or spirit." Furthermore, the *sunsum* is capable of leaving the body at night when one is sleeping and of being "attacked by evil images." But, unlike the *kra*, the *sunsum* returns not to the Samanadze but to the phylogenetic paternal spirit (*egyabosom*) to await possible reincarnation.

Besides the fact that in Christensen's systematization the woman is reduced to an instrument of procreation, another contentious point raised by Christensen has to do with blood in relation to the father. Men, of course, do not transmit blood as he maintains, otherwise the whole matrilineal system of descent to which the Akan people adhere would be a sham. It is true that the Akan people to the south were influenced by Europeans more so than those to the north, but that did not alter the matrilineal system of descent.

Arguing from a socio-historical perspective, I. Chukwukere [15] refutes Christensen's thesis on historical grounds. Chukwukere contends that Christensen puts too much emphasis on "functional classification" in the attempt to discover an appropriate name for the Mfantse "social system." Chukwukere particularly dismisses Christensen's assertion that the father's blood is "stronger" than the mother's. This line of reasoning, he points out, is the direct result of "patrilineal white aliens."

Robert Lystad[16] offers a socio-theological basis for the personality. Working among the people of Goaso in the late 1940s and early 1950s, Lystad conceived of the *kra* as a "supernatural soul" first placed in the primordial man by God, Nyame. Since then it has been passed down from fathers to their children. It is the *kra* of the man that imparts life to the woman's blood to form the human being, thus forming the basis for the matrilineal system of descent. The *kra* assumes not only a new life-form after death but also a new name, *saman,* residing with the Asamanfo at Asamando (ancestral world)—meaning, the *kra* is endowed with immortality. Furthermore, the *sasa* is the restless soul in limbo.

Lystad thought of the *sunsum*, which originates with the father, as a functionary of the *kra*. The role of the *sunsum*, then, is that of a "protector or escort of the soul and the person." But unlike the eternal *kra*, the sunsum dies with the body. Humans share the *kra* and the sunsum together with plants and animals. However, the deities possess heavier or superior *asunsum* (plural) than humans.

Like Christensen, Lystad ascribes the *kra* and *sunsum* to the father, thus making the father the giver of life. But, unlike Christensen, Lystad adheres to the notion that the blood originates with the mother, a position shared both by Rattray and Field.

The position advanced by Eva L. R. Meyerowitz [17] is that the *kra* originates with Nyame, the moon or "Mother-goddess." The essential nature of God, the Mother-goddess, is fire, "the life-giving spirit" that brought about the birth of the universe.[18] The world is the very *kra* of Nyame. The *kra* of Nyame is fire and the fire-*kra* of a woman that is shot "into the blood-stream of men, beasts and plants," thereby giving life to all life forms. The basis for the femininity of the fire-*kra* is its red color (blood), making it inherently female and the *kra* of the Mother-goddess. The *kra* is eternal, so that when a person dies it returns to its source and awaits reincarnation into the same family via *honhom,* the "breath of divine life." In fact, the *honhom* is an intrinsic part of the *kra*, giving the *kra* its vitality.

The *sunsum* Meyerowitz defines as "character," "personality," and "destiny." The nature of the personality is predicated upon the seven natal days of the week in which one is born. The natal days are derived from the seven planetary systems—Moon, Monday; Mars, Tuesday; Mercury, Wednesday; Jupiter, Thursday; Venus, Friday; Saturn, Saturday; Sun, Sunday. In other words, the planets have direct bearing on the *sunsum* of a person so as to shape the individual's character, personality, and destiny. At death the sunsum is transformed into saman (shade) and journeys to the samandow (ancestral world) below the earth. Another meaning of the sunsum is shadow, although after death it is called saman, the "likeness" or "reflexion" of the personality of the deceased.

The position advanced by Meyerowitz concerning the *kra* is antithetical to Lystad's. For Meyerowitz, it is the mother who imparts life to men, not the father as Lystad asserts. She concurs with Field and Lystad, however, that the *kra* is not, as Rattray asserts, exclusively human.

Meyerowitz's assertion that the Akan people conceive of the *kra* as fire is incorrect. This position is not shared by any of the ethnographers discussed. Moreover, her attempt to create an Akan cosmogony out of this fire-*kra* phenomenon is alien to the Akan people, as we will see below.

The first real attempt by an Akan scholar to respond to foreign ethnographers comes from J. B. Danquah.[19] From the ethical standpoint he tries to offer the ontological basis for the personality, and dismisses the Christian notion of "original sin." He maintains that the human being is the very *okara* or soul of God, endowed with *nkra* or intelligence. The problem, however, is that evil exists in the human being.

To Danquah, the personality is essentially of two components, namely, the *sunsum* and the *okara*. The *sunsum*, he posits, is the covering of the body, encasing the *okara*. Thus the sunsum protects and guides the soul, the unadulterated essence of God in the human being.[20] The *sunsum* is the physical end-product of a developmental process commencing with *E-su* or nature, the "prime genetic basis for the origin of the social subject, i.e., man." He goes on to elaborate on his developmental scheme by saying:

> The individual, as *e-su*, having broken away from the unformed mass of the race, presents himself to Nyankopon for *nkrabea* or his purposed decree, thereby acquiring *hyebea*, the *e-su's* soul or *okara*, namely, the distinctive capacities of a truly human being with a corresponding responsibility to realize those capacities.[21]

During the divine episode the *esu* is impregnated with a soul by God. Then, born into the corporeal world, the soul becomes the *sunsum*, the reflection of God by virtue of the *esu* (nature, quality, character, essence). The *sunsum*, as matter, is the "superstructure" of the personality and therefore different from the body or *onipadua* composed of blood. Once in the world the *sunsum* must attain the *esu*, which is often unattainable because of evil in the *sunsum*. Although the *sunsum* is not evil inherently, it nonetheless acquires evil during the maturational process. However, the *sunsum* is not opposed to the *okara*, rather it is a "conscious counterpart of *okara*" that offers itself as the attainable.

Like the *sunsum*, the *okara* emanates from God. In the human being, however, it manifests itself as *honhom*, "the spirit of pure ethereality that...links up man with the Ideal Spirit, pure Honhom." The *okara* is "intelligence," endowed with a decree—*nkrabea-hyebea*—by God, making it impossible for evil to exist in the *okara*. Therefore failure to achieve perfection existentially (because of evil in the *sunsum*) means that the *okara* must be reincarnated to continue from where it left off until such time as the good is consummated. That is to say, an individual's ethical existence or *obara* is meritoriously computed during the life cycles until the individual accrues the highest good.

The *honhom* and the *okara* are inseparable. The *honhom* is that refined spirit of vitality of the *okara* in every human being; it is the "spirit of ultimate being" that permeates every reality. In fact, reality *is* *honhom*. Furthermore, the *okara* encompasses what Danquah calls *nkrabea-hyebea*, a sort of double destiny or decree from God. This decree is what gives purpose to every human being in the world. Hence Danquah's teleological cyclical scheme is expressed as follows:

e-su → *nkrabea-hyebea* → *okara* → *honhom* → *sunsum* →

The problem with Danquah's scheme is his rendition of the *okra-nkra* as intelligence. (The term for "intelligence" is *nyansa* and not *okra* or *nkra*). However, he is right in positing that intelligence is divine in origin, that is, that the *okra* is endowed with intelligence. Danquah simply overstates his position. His conceptual rendition of the sunsum is closer to Lystad's.

K. A. Busia,[22] in his essay, "The Ashanti," takes a political perspective on the personality. He argues that the human being essentially has two components: the biological, represented by *mogya* (blood) and derived from the mother; and the *ntoro* (spirit), derived from the father. He posits that the physical component, in this case blood of the mother, establishes a mother-child bond and lays the foundation for the matrilineal system of descent by the Akan. These blood groupings are traceable to a common matrix, but most important they bestow "status and membership with the lineage...and rights and obligations as a citizen."

On the spiritual side of the personality, Busia utilizes the *ntoro* and the *sunsum* synonymously, even though the *sunsum* is derived from the generic, *ntoro*. He defines the *sunsum* as the "ego," "personality," and "distinctive character" of a person. For him, it is finite and ends with the demise of the person. The father, Busia avers, transmits his *sunsum* to his children during sexual intercourse with their mother, so that the *ntoro-sunsum* "moulds the child's personality and disposition. The...child cannot thrive if his father's *sunsum* is alienated...." To be "molded in the father's *sunsum*" means that the child shares in the father's service to any of the twelve generic *ntoro* groupings.

In addition to the physical and spiritual composition of the personality, Busia discusses a third component. During copulation, God endows the union with a part of God, the *kra*, or "life force" of every person. Consequently, every individual is imbued with an infinite quality of God, the *kra*, distinctively apart from the father's, and which returns to God upon the individual's demise. Of course, both the *ntoro-sunsum* and the *kra* need the blood of the mother for the creative process to be realized.

Busia differs with Danquah on the provenance of the sunsum. For Busia the father is the source of the *sunsum* which he transmits to his offspring through copulation. Danquah, however, maintains that it originates with God. To Busia, the father, the mother, and God all contribute to the formation of the human being.

Kofi Antubam[23] adheres to the view that the personality has three main components. First, the material component, *mbogya* (blood), derived from the mother; second, a spiritual component called *ntoro-sunsum* or "self or ego," originating with the father; and the *okara* (soul) having its provenance with God. The *okara*, moreover, serves as an anchorage for conscience (*tibowaa*) and influences all human activity. The *okara* in action is when one adjudicates sincerely and honestly. Intrinsic to the *okara* are the *nkrabea* (the brief message of life) and the *honhom* (breath).

But Antubam takes the personality a step further aesthetically. For the body to be considered beautiful it must fall within certain geometric configurations. These geometric expressions are either masculine—circle, rectangle, square, even number, full moon, chevron, concentric, and four-angled star; or feminine—triangle, oval, egg, paw-paw, odd number, crescent moon, waves, spironic circle, and five-angled star.

For the individual to be healed completely, it is imperative that the healer tackle both the spiritual and the physical facets of the personality. The psychosomatic, spiritual perspective is espoused by Kofi Appiah-Kubi.[24] He identifies three sources that contribute to the formation of a holistic personality. These sources are: God, the mother, and the father. From God comes the *okra* on the day of the week the individual is born. The *okra* is imbued with immortality and upon the demise of the individual departs to "join the spirit world." In addition to the *okra*, God gives *nkrabea* or destiny. The *nkrabea* is very enigmatic, making life capriciously hard. Existentially, it is often used to explain whatever station in life the individual finds himself or herself in, although the individual does not resign herself or himself to an unproductive state of existence.

The physical form of the personality is made up of the mother's *mogya* (blood), while the father provides the individual's *sunsum* or spirit. The *sunsum*, Appiah-Kubi defines relationally. That is, the child comes under the aegis of the father's *sunsum*, something the child needs if it is to stay healthy.

Spurred by his monthly discussions on aspects of the Akan culture Kwesi Sarpong[25] wrote several articles dealing with different issues, including the personality concept. Sarpong maintains that the components of the personality are traceable to the mother, the father, and God. The person receives from the mother *bogya* (blood); from the father, *sunsum*; and from God, *okra* (soul) and *honhom* (breath of life).

The disposition of a person is traceable to the *sunsum* because it is the *sunsum* of the father that "moulds the child making him what he is: kind, stupid, eloquent, clever, fluent, lazy, hardworking, as the case maybe." This is why the father's *sunsum-ntoro* should not be alienated, for to do so may cause illness to the child.

The nature of the *okra* is thought by Sarpong to be a "small particle of God." Upon the death of a person the *okra* returns to its provenance—God. The *okra*, however, is accompanied by a "double destiny" and *honhom*, defined as that which enables one to breathe and makes one a living person. Subsequently, the cessation of *honhom* means death.

Kofi Asare Opoku [26] argues that the human being is a composite of the *okra* (soul), the sunsum or "an intangible element" necessary for character (suban), *ntoro* or "inherited characteristics," and *mogya* (blood). The *okra* is imbued with immortality and departs at the time of death to God. Opoku asserts, moreover, that the *okra* is uniquely human.[27] Before it departs from God to the mundane world it is entrusted with an immutable *nkrabea* or *hyebea* (destiny). Consequently, the *kra* is thought of as "bearer of destiny." The process of actualization of destiny in the world is what Opoku calls *obra* or *obrabo*.

The *sunsum* is perceived developmentally from light to heavy in relation to maturation. It is thought of ethically in relation to a person's disposition and intelligence. The *sunsum*, unlike the *okra* which "remains within a person," is imbued with locomotion, enabling it to depart the body during the dream state and "may or may not return" to the body. The reason is that a light *sunsum* may be vulnerable to attacks by a more developed *sunsum*, causing a person to be ill.

Closely akin to *sunsum* is *ntoro*, derived from the father. Until puberty the child comes under the aegis of its father's *ntoro*, at which point the child's own *ntoro* assumes greater control of his or her own characteristics.

The final entity of Opoku's scheme is *mogya* (blood), the material aspect of the person and the basis for the ebusua or *nton* system of descent. When a person dies the assumption is that the *blood* goes to "Mother Earth."

The philosophical perspective has been presented by Kwame Gyekye.[28] In his view the personality is made up of different components, one of which is the very essence or "spark" of God, *okra* (soul). Explaining the basis for the *okra* as immortal, life-imparting agent, Gyekye utilizes the term, "*okratseasefo*" to mean a "living soul". The *okra* is also imbued with destiny or *nkrabea*.

Gyekye also examines the relationship between the *okra* and *honhom*. Although closely aligned, they are separate entities, nonetheless. He explicates: "the departure of the soul from the body means the death of a person, and so does the cessation of breath. Yet this does not mean that the *honhom* (breath) is the same as the *okra* (soul). It is the *okra* that 'causes' the breathing. Thus, the *honhom* is the tangible manifestation or evidence of the presence of the *okra*."[29]

Concerning the *sunsum* (spirit) Gyekye presents the argument for the divine origin of this phenomenon. He defines the *sunsum* as the "basis of a man's personality, and,...'his ego'" or the "activating principle." On the basis of this definition he cast doubt on the corporeal source of the *sunsum*. He argues: "Thus, if the *sunsum* is that which constitutes the basis of an individual's personality, it cannot be a physical thing, for qualities like courage, jealousy, gentleness, forcefulness, and dignity are psychological, not sensible or physical. The conception of personality as the function of the *sunsum* makes a material conception of the latter logically impossible." The fact that the *sunsum* is the character in dreams and is an "active part" of the *okra*, means that the *sunsum* is divine.

But there seems to be a problem between the *sunsum* and the *ntoro.* The *ntoro,* Gyekye contends, is transmitted by the father as "inherited characteristics." The difference between the *sunsum* and the *ntoro* is their respective points of origination.

Having demonstrated the divine natures of the *sunsum* and the *okra,* Gyekye then discusses the material components. The physical component of the personality is that which is derived from the mother as blood. The body is related to the *okra,* also believed to be blood, the "physical or rather physiological 'medium' for the soul." This means that there is unity of soul and body, ensuring inter-spiritual-physical "causal influence" on the *okra* and *honam* (body). This, then, is the basis for holistic healing.

N o t e s

1. See P. de Marees, *Description and Historical Account of the Gold Kingdom of Guinea (1602)* (The Oxford Univ. Press, 1987).
2. Ibid., 28-30.
3. A. B. Ellis, *The Tshi-speaking Peoples of the Gold Coast of West Africa* (Chapman & Hall, Ltd., 1887).
4. Ibid., p. 149.
5. Ibid., pp. 157-167.
6. See R. S. Rattray, *Ashanti* (Oxford: Clarendon Press, 1923).
7. Ibid., p. 36.
8. Ibid.
9. See M. J. Field, *Akim-Kotoku: An Oman of the Gold Coast* (London: The Crown Agents for the Colonies, 1948).
10. Ibid., pp. 161-162.
11. See M. J. Field, *Search for Security: An Ethno-Psychiatric Study of Rural Ghana* (London: Faber & Faber, 1960).
12. Ibid., pp. 27-28.
13. Ibid., p. 119.
14. See J. B. Christensen, *Double Descent Among the Fanti* (New Haven: Human Relations Area Files, 1954).
15. I. Chukwukere, "Akan Theory of Conception—Are the Fante Really Aberrant" *Africa* 48, 2 1978:135-148.
16. R. Lystad, *The Ashanti: A Proud People* (New Brunswick: Rutgers Univ. Press, 1958) p. 155.
17. E. L. R. Meyerowitz, *The Akan of Ghana: Their Ancient Beliefs* (London: Faber & Faber, Ltd., 1958).
18. Ibid., pp. 23-24.

19. J. B. Danquah, *The Akan Doctrine of God* (London: Frank Cass & Co., Ltd., [1944] 1968), pp. 5-42.
20. Ibid., pp. 66-67.
21. Ibid., p. 111.
22. K. A. Busia, "The Ashanti," in Daryll Forde (ed.), *African Worlds: Studies in the Cosmological and Social Values of African Peoples* (London Oxford Univ. Press, 1954), pp. 190-209.
23. K. Antubam, *Ghana's Heritage of Culture* (Leipzig: Koehler & Amelang, 1963), pp. 36-39.
24. K. Appiah-Kubi, *Man Cures, God Heals* (New York: Friendship Press, 1981), pp. 5-17.
25. K. Sarpong, *Ghana in Retrospect* (Tema: Ghana Publ. Corp., 1974) pp. 37-44.
26. K. A. Opoku, *West African Traditional Religion* (Accra: FEP, Int. Private Ltd., 1978) pp. 94-100.
27. Opoku posits that animals have what he calls sasa.
28. K. Gyekye, *An Essay on African Philosophical Thought: The Akan Conceptual Scheme* (Cambridge: Cambridge Univ. Press, 1987), 85- 128.
29. Ibid., p. 88.

Chapter 3

THE OLD WOMAN AND HER CHILDREN

As I sat anxiously waiting for Archbishop Tutu—the commencement speaker for my graduating class—to speak, I heard the president of the university say in reference to Mary Leakey, the famous paleontologist, who was being honored by Emory University, that because of her work we now know that humanity originated with a single woman in Africa. But what has taken scientists a long time to affirm, the Akan and other African peoples have always believed.

So what do the Akan believe about the beginning? To talk about the beginning it is imperative to begin with a point of reference. For, within this context lies all that there was, is, and will be. But most importantly, the beginning deals with a people and their cultural heritage, including religion, philosophy, socio-political organization, economic, and, above all, their spiritual concerns. By spirituality I mean the quest by a people to aspire to the original, ideal epoch that has been superseded by impermanence.

I have chosen the Akan cosmogony as a point of reference because it offers me an inclusive, paradigmatic platform from which to speak to the quest for meaning and spirituality. The Akan creation story[1] itself is brief, yet what the elders have handed down by word of mouth contains enough information to constitute a people——the Akan. The key to the story, as to every sacred tradition in Akan society, is the ability to decipher what has been handed down to succeeding generations.

The first qualitative act of Nana Nyame, the Akan monotheistic God, is God's creativity. That is, in the beginning Nana Nyame alone created heaven or the sky (*osor*), the earth (*asase*), and order (*adze nyinaa Nyame ahyihye no pepeeper*) instantaneously.

There are two things to be noted about the creative act of Nana Nyame. First is the unilateral creativity of Nana Nyame. In the Yoruba cosmogony, by contrast, Olodumare (God), assisted by the divinity Orisha-nla, created the world in four days and on the fifth day rested. We find a similar motif running through the Judeo-Christian traditions. The point here is not whether or not God created alone or with assistance, but rather what socio-political foundations were set up as a result of a particular cosmogony. In the case of the Yoruba people the socio-political structure is patrilineally based, whereas the Akan is matrilineally based, as we will see below.

Secondly, to say that Nana Nyame has arranged everything accordingly does not mean predestination, but rather order and foreknowledge of everything. The Calvinist view of predestination is not a notion compatible with the Akan world view, because of the Akan conception of reincarnation that leads to a universal salvation for every one.

The foreknowledge of Nana Nyame means that God has advance knowledge of how things will turn out for everyone. This is possible because God is the originator of what everyone would accomplish even before one is born. The Akan people call this phenomenon *nkrabea*, a concept to be explored in detail in Chapter 5.

For the Akan people to the south, the earth came into existence on a Friday; for those to the north, on a Thursday. Hence the earth is called *Asase Efua* and *Asase Yaa,* respectively. On these two days the Akan people may not till the earth because this period of time is devoted to consecrating the earth. Any acts that desecrate the earth must be avoided. These may include spilling blood (homicide) on her, sexual indiscretion on the open field, toxic waste, and indiscriminate use of land.

When I was growing up I heard many versions of the same creation account. But no matter how many versions I heard, the essential nature of the story remained unchanged. That is, in addition to God's creativity, God lived in the sky, though not the sky. The sky was very close to the earth, occupied by an old woman and her children. We are not told how many children or who fathered them, but it would not be wrong to conjecture that Nana Nyame was the father. Also, based on the constellation called *Abrewa na ni mba* (the Old Woman and Her Children), we know that the children are six in number. When the Old Woman herself is counted as one of the stars, then the number augments to seven. This number corresponds with the seven matrilineal divisions of the Akan people.

The only food the Old Woman and her children ate was *fufu*.[2] But whenever she prepared her meal the pestle would strike God, meaning she and her children could reach God whenever necessary. This went on for a long time until one day God asked her to stop or God would move to a higher sphere. But God's demands fell on deaf ears and rightly so since she and her children had to eat. So one day God ascended higher so that the pestle was unable to reach anymore.

Undaunted by God's action the Old Woman instructed her children to pile up all the mortars they could find. Her aim was to restore the lost proximity to God and she almost succeeded. It got to a point where only one mortar was needed to reach God, and after a futile search for the last mortar she instructed her children to remove the original mortar at the bottom of the pile to be placed on top. This, of course, proved to be a tragic blunder because as soon as the mortar was removed the pile collapsed and injured some of her children.

The aim of the creation story is didactic. Children like myself are taught many ethical and moral lessons, including the origin of death, suffering, diseases, as well as obedience and respect for the elders. To be disobedient is to suffer the same fate as the Old Woman and her children.

As a youngster I accepted this lesson at face value, but later in my adult life I realized that it taught more than the unconditional obedience to the elders. This mythology contains the ontological basis for theology and religion, anthropology, philosophy, and socio-political rights and citizenry.

Existentially, the ideal community was headed by the Old Woman who taught her children everything there was to know. Politically the throne or stool belongs to her and only her children and the children of her female descendants must ascend the throne. Thus the matrilineal system of descent practiced by the Akan people was established.

Of course, the creation story is beyond time and space. No one can really say when and where this divine drama took place, except that it is as real as the earth is solid. It seems that when these archetypal models, that is, Nana Nyame and the Old Woman have established the paradigms for existence for their children, they simply *disappeared*. In fact, Akan mythology speaks about giants whose responsibilities were simply to originate certain occupation models for humanity; once they had accomplished this, they died.

Two of these giants (actually three) were Kow Egya and Asabu Amanfi (and his sister, Amanfua). The former established fishing while the latter introduced farming. I visited or passed through the town of Asabu, where Asabu Amanfi was king, many times on my way to Asuansi Farm Institute, where I was a student in 1975.

If God had a name, then what about his female counterpart? *Abrewa* was her name, as noted above. We also know that the earth is emblematic of her in the same way that the sky is emblematic of God. Asona is believed to be her daughter, the first of seven matrilineal families. The rest are: Tweedan, Kona, Anana, Abradze, Asakyir, and Asenee. Each matrilineal family is identified by a totemic symbol that may differ from one locale to the next.

Asona, some accounts say, evolved from the fox (*Oso*) into the most beautiful woman on earth. The question may be asked: Is the fox the same as the Old Woman? What we know, however, is that the fox and the crow, domesticated by Asona and given the white collar by Baawah, Asona's daughter, are the two major totemic symbols for the Asona matrilineal family. Concerning Asona herself, it is often said that the back of her head was even more beautiful than the most beautiful person on earth.

One day the archetypal community discovered a pot full of gold, but coiled around the pot was a snake. Everyone of the matrilineal families was afraid to retrieve the gold. But Asona made a decision to retrieve it, telling her brother that she would rather retrieve the gold for her children and be bitten, than bequeath nothing to them at her old age. True, she was bitten and afterwards died, but not until she brought the gold to her children. Hence, it is said of the Asona *ebusua* that they hustle for a course (Asona *wonpir kwa*)

Theologically the creation story alludes to the conception of a "fall" of humanity and the repercussions thereof. That is, an eternal epoch was superseded by mortality, depravation, and impoverishment, resulting in the quest for restoration of immortality. For the Akan people, the attainment of ancestorhood is tantamount to the ideal era when humans lived eternally face-to-face with the Old Woman and her children and Nana Nyame.

However, unlike Eve in the Judeo-Christian creation account and the "fall," the Akan Old Woman is not reviled or vilified for causing or bringing about death. If anything, she was worshipped and rightly so because she taught her children all that there is to know. She was an indefatigably courageous woman who did everything for her children, whether pursuing Nana Nyame or risking her life for her children in order to bring them the best.

In attempting to reach God by piling up the mortars she proved that, yes, Nana Nyame could be reached, but not in the flesh. Oneness with Nana Nyame could only take place in death, as God is also death.[3] The collapse of the mortars goes to show that at the highest spiritual stage, which is tantamount to oneness with God existentially, the final leap is achieved through death. This is imperative because the earth-mother must receive what is hers, the body.

Furthermore the Old Woman is thought to be all-wise, omniscient, and just. Consequently, during adjudication the elders would often times reach an impasse. And when that happens, certain elders would be chosen and excused from the council to go and deliberate. But before they left, they would say to the remainder of the council: "We are going to consult with the Old Woman." Similarly, upon their return they would say to the waiting elders: "We have consulted with the Old Woman, and this is her verdict...." And why not? She was the only one her children saw and taught them language; it is consistent that when her children have reached an impasse they would turn to the one who is the quintessence of language. With old age also comes wisdom, knowledge, and experience, hence her omniscience. And as the first judge over her children, she always corrects every injustice that arises among her children. Thus, where inequities prevail the Akan people turn to her to settle all inequities.

Celestially the Old Woman also figures prominently. She is featured in a constellation called *Abrewa na ni mba* (The Old Woman and Her Children). The constellation is led by the "old woman" star, followed immediately by three stars, who in turn are followed by three more stars.[4] The relationship between the *Abrewa na ni mba* and the Akan people is that her appearance heralds abundance. She appears from the south or south-east and makes her way across the sky and sets to the north. In other words, she emerges from the sea and journeys toward land along with a plethora of fish from cold to warmer waters landward. When she is spotted, fishermen do not engage in deep water fishing. She makes her apparition generally in the month of July during the wee hours of the morning. Consequently, she is called the beneficent mother (*obaatan*) because she knows the needs of her children (*obaatan na onyim dzaa ne mba bedzi*).

Besides the *Abrewa na ni mba*, perhaps the most well-known of these stars is a nuptial star called *Kyekye pe awar* (Kyekye, the ideal bride). There are romantic songs praising her unwavering commitment and devotion to marriage. She is never seen alone but together with the crescent moon believed to be the husband, brother, and son. Some diadems depict this royal marriage to symbolize the dual occupancy of the Akan royal throne. If there is a single stellar object that reigns supreme in the consciousness of the Akan people, it is the *Bosom* (Moon). The moon is regarded as the ultimate *Nana* or king. As king he rules on behalf of his mother, wife, and sister. Together, *Kyekye pe awar* and the crescent moon represent the ideal ancestors of the Akan people.

The sighting of the new moon by the Akan people is a cause for celebration. It instills a sense of continuum and hope in the future of humanity. The spotting of the crescent moon evokes shouts like: "Nana, seeing you is life for me," "Nana, take away all my ills and misfortunes," and "Nana, I will be alive a year from now." These statements demonstrate that the moon takes upon itself the evils of the humanity, dies with them, and resurrects in the form of the crescent moon as life giver.

These shouts of praise towards the moon are indicative of the Old Woman's children reaching out to their father, God. The basis for this is the saying that: "All are the children of Nana Nyame; none is the child of the earth." The earth, too, aspires to her husband. The whole of creation aspires to the sky, the abode of Nana Nyame. Reciprocating in kind, Nana Nyame embraces the earth, his mother, sister, and wife and children in the form of the crescent moon. In the larger context the dome of the sky is indicative of the embrace of the whole universe by God. Existentially, the story of God, the primordial Old Woman, and Her Children points to a conception of community. That is, the archetypal woman and her children were the first community or *ebusua*. In practice the *ebusua* is the uterine, consanguineous linear group that congregates to bury the dead and share funeral expenses. The *ebusua* sets the date for the final funeral obsequies, appoint a successor for the deceased, and remembers the deceased on the eighth day, the second week, the fortieth day, the eightieth day, and the one year anniversary. Comprised of individuals who until brought together for a meeting pursue their individual endeavors, the *ebusua* does not really exist until members converge. In this way the *ebusua* is the extended unit of the family, and members of an *ebusua* are siblings (*anua-nom*).

After introducing every African who visited the church I ministered as either my "brother" or my "sister," a church member ask me: "Rev., how many brothers and sisters do you have in Africa?" In turn I ask him why he referred to every African American male as "brother" and every female as "sister." I demanded to know where he thought the practice originated. Since the Akan people really do not have separate words for "sister" and "brother," the neuter *nua* (sibling) communicates fidelity, comradery, blood relation, and a strong sense of belonging. Consequently, to break faith is tantamount to betrayal of the entire family, the *ebusua*.

In current practice, the best moment to observe the *ebusua* at work is during funerals. It is said that the *ebusua* loves even its dead as they gather to bury one of their own with wailing and pomp. Therefore, it is the civic, political, economic, and religious duty of every member to journey from far and near with the single aim of interring their matrikin folks. At funerals the totemic symbol is placed on the compound where the *ebusua* has gathered. The totemic symbol identifies for the larger community the *ebusua* to which the deceased belonged.

More than just social observance, it is the blood of the mother herself that binds the individual to his or her *ebusua*. It is genetically impossible to divorce oneself from this belonging. The individual embodies blood by virtue of the fact that the material aspect of personality is composed of it. The inanimate body (blood) is then combined with other elements from God and the father into what the Akan call a living being. Even though the living being is one among the human family, his or her allegiance and primary responsibilities are to the *ebusua*.

In this way an individual needn't purchase death insurance, as the *ebusua* would claim the corpse for burial. However, every person is required to contribute monetarily for the up-keep of the *ebusua*. Otherwise the children of the deceased would be obliged to pay all outstanding dues before the *ebusua* accepts and inters a body. Nostalgically, a former parishioner remarked to me: "Reverend, this was the way we use to take care of our dead and our selves, but now we don't have the family anymore."

From the structural standpoint the tangible component of the personality (blood) is metaphorically referred to as a tree (*dua*). Hence the individual is known as a living tree. The tree metaphor is derived from God, the ultimate dependable tree, *Tweduapon*. However, there is a difference between Nana Nyame as the tree and the human being as a tree, in this respect: God is incorruptible, immutable, and infinite while humans are corruptible and finite.

The metaphor of tree and forest can be extended in observation of nature. Anyone conversant with the forest will concur that it is not uncommon to observe one huge, tall, stout tree towering over many trees or shrubs. After a storm it may be discovered that the smaller trees are either leaning or have fallen on the super tree. After a few days the trees may find enough resilience to restore themselves to upright positions. This illustrates the close rapport between God and humans. Although human beings will fall and die, they do so on God, the unmoved, dependable, and infinite tree. Whenever a person dies the euphemistic expression is that a tree has fallen. Yet it is unambiguously understood that a person, especially a king, never dies.

The symbolic reference to the individual as a tree, as de Marees has noted, further evokes images of aestheticism. From the structural standpoint, Antubam contends that the ideally beautiful person's body must be configured as follows:

> Looking at the body from the side or front, the shape of the head and of the neck from the top of the head to the end of the chin must appear like an egg with the wider portion uppermost. Looking at it from the side, the head must sit on the neck at an angle of about thirty five degrees with the top part falling back. This falling back...has an optical effect on the viewer. For, thrown into perspective, so to say, wide, the top part of the face grows wider and gives a larger appearance from the front. This is, perhaps, what the traditional Akan Ghanaian carver is trying to express in the head of the female *Akuaba* (fertility and play doll). Again, to be beautiful, the head must fix into the neck at a point a little below the head to the bottom line of the chin.[5]

He continues:

> The neck which should have wrinkles or rings on it must fall into an elongated oval shape with the smaller part of it tapering towards the head. The wrinkles or rings here must be at odd number when counted to be a perfect beauty. The torso, starting from the shoulder line or collarbone to the waist line, must appear an oval from the larger part towards the neck. The thighs from the waist line to the bottom of the knee cap must look like an egg with the wider portion towards the waist. This requirement...makes...men...like substantial thighs and buttocks. And...ladies...push their buttocks out to form a concave at the back of the waist in order to appear beautiful. And, their tight western dress stresses this point.... Their legs, from centre of the knee cap to the ground level, must appear oval with the wider part towards the knee. The feet, when put together, must fall in a good space of an oval with its wider part towards the toes.[6]

The fertility doll alluded to by Antubam is indicative of the ideal Akan woman. One morning my wife called me to come and listen to the news on television. Featured on the *Good Morning America* news show were some women with their babies in their arms. Their story was that they and many others——fourteen women in all——got pregnant by touching a fertility doll that was placed at the entrance to the office they worked. My wife remarked: "What is extraordinary about this; we have always believed in the doll in Africa!" But I responded by saying that now, at least, our belief in the *Akua-ba* is no longer viewed as a superstition.

For Akan women the fertility doll or Akua-ba is believed to have supernatural powers to cause barren women to be pregnant. Women looking to be pregnant would touch, play with, and carry the Akua-ba on their backs. Others would have their children, daughters in particular, play with the doll so that they would not only assume the aestheticism of the doll but also its nature as the ideal woman.

Perhaps the most compelling expression of the tree metaphor is the reference to the *ebusua* as a tree stand. The *ebusua* is described as a grouping of trees viewed from the perspective of the whole, but upon a closer view is found to be composed of single trees. In other words, the *ebusua* only exists *en masse (ebusua ye dom)*. And the events that bring about the return to collective solidarity are funerals, elections, festivals, and crises.

The Akan people use other metaphors from nature to relate to the corporeal nature of the personality. Just as the tree has a bark, so the individual has an outer covering called *noho*. Underneath the outer covering or skin is the flesh or body (*honam*). There is a slight distinction between the flesh and skin for the simple reason that they have separate names. However, their symbiosis allow for the *homan* to be rendered as body or skin.

The question of whether or not women or men transmitted blood was raised by Rattray. As a European, Rattray could not conceptualize an anthropological world view different from his. He was particularly puzzled by the fact that it was women, and not men as Europeans believe, who transmitted blood to their offspring among the Akan people. And upon repeated attempts to learn more about this phenomenon, the Asante women offered him the evidence. Rattray writes:

> The raison d'etre given by the Ashanti for tracing *bogya* (blood) through the female line alone is to be found in certain physiological conditions which they observed, i.e. the presence of blood at childbirth and during menstruation. The presence of blood on these occasions has given rise to the supposition that 'blood alone can be transmitted by and through a female.'

While discussing this matter with three women,..., I asked why, if a male had blood in his body, as they acknowledged he had, he could not then transmit it to his offspring. I have indeed repeatedly asked this question and always been told such a thing was impossible and had never been heard of. On this occasion the answer was that 'if a male transmitted his blood through the penis he could not beget a child.' I can conceive no possible answer that would show more clearly the underlying belief in the minds of these people, but if further evidence is needed, then the fact that the word for the male-transmitted *ntoro* (spirit), seems sometimes used in the sense of semen supplies the proof.[7]

The source of the blood that forms the individual has its provenance in the ancestral world. The Akan people believe that every child born is sent or *willed* by a spiritual mother who resides at the ancestral abode (Samanadze) called *Na-Saman* (mother Saman). That is, just as everyone has a mother in the world, every Akan has a mother in the ancestral world.

The very mentioning of the Na-Saman conjures up the primordial mother in the creation myth and her children. And the question is whether or not the spiritual mother is the one and the same woman in the creation account. For one thing, it confirms the fact that the conception of the *ebusua* has its truest incipience in the spiritual world, Samanadze, the ideal world of the ancestors.

The Na-Saman "sends" children into the world in the same way that a mother gives birth. She inculcates her children as to what she expects of them, the duration of stay in the world, and if sent to find a person or retrieve an item, where to locate it. It is believed that some children are born with the sole purpose of seeking wealth for the spiritual mother. And once in the world they may die summarily in accordance with what the Na-Saman has mandated.

The Akan people believe that many unexplained phenomena transpire in the spiritual realm of the ancestors before they are actually manifested in the flesh or mundane realm. To them the spiritual always supersedes the mundane because the spiritual embodies ultimate reality while the world and all human activities are mimicry of the spiritual. This leads me to explore the concept of reincarnation. If it sounds simplistic to ask the question: Where do babies come from? then perhaps it is equally naive to ask: Where do people go after death?

No matter how childish such questions may seem, the fundamental key to understanding the cyclical notion of life has its beginnings with these questions. If I were to offer a straightforward answer, I would say that babies originate from and return to the spiritual, ancestral world.

A woman I saw on television one day told about dying at a hospital and leaving her children behind. She believes she is now that woman reincarnated in search of her children. Among other things, she meticulously talked about where she used to live in Ireland, the hospital she died in, even the Catholic church she attended. These flashbacks eventually took her back to Ireland where her children, now old, collaborated her story and reclaimed their once-dead mother.

The conception of reincarnation is inextricably tied to both the mundane and the spiritual worlds. The premier of the two worlds is the spiritual because it is the ideal abode of the ancestors whereas the mundane is only a model of the ideal, as Plato has also noted.

Every ethnic group has its own reference to the conception of reincarnation. This is also true of Africa, and particularly the Akan people. I have heard my mother contradict herself many times. She would say when frustrated that she will not reincarnate again. However, in appreciation for what someone has done for her she will fancifully say to that person that she will reincarnate into that person's family. What is obvious is that a person can *choose* to reincarnate to fulfill his or her purpose in being.

The elders and the ancestors reserve the right to reincarnate anywhere around the world and into any race of their choice. However, most people reincarnate into their own families in order to complete their purpose of being, or to retrieve something they may have left behind in the world. If the reincarnated one is looking for a person, it will recognize the person as soon as it lay eyes on him or her.

But is there any compelling cause pertinent to this phenomenon? The Akan people believe that every child born is sent or *willed* by an archetypal mother who resides in the ancestral world. That is, just as everyone has a mother in the mundane world, so everyone has a mother in the spiritual world. Specifically, the spiritual mother "sends" children into the world in the same way a mother gives birth. Prior to birth, however, the unborn child is inculcated by its spiritual mother as to what she expects of it, its duration of stay in the world, and, if sent to retrieve something, where to locate it. Sometimes the spiritual mother sends her children simply to taunt and inflict pain on a couple by dying soon after birth. The poignancy of the natural parent's grief brings delight to the spiritual mother, who rewards her children upon their deaths.

The way couples experiencing cyclical sudden infant deaths end this phenomenon is to inflict pain and punishment on the corpse. The family may smear the corpse with hot spices, make cuts on the face or body, or simply revile it. In most instances the corpse is interred ignominiously and without any pomp. The aim here is for the natural parents to reciprocate in kind what the spiritual mother first willed through her child in relation to its worldly parents. However, couples who lose their children for the first time do not mourn them because the poignancy of their grief may engender barrenness.

No one will deny the residual emotional pain after the loss of a child, but it is equally said that the woman who is impregnated shortly after such a loss takes solace from it. The resultant conception is thought to be the dead child who has reincarnated after being shunned by its spiritual mother. Babies reincarnated, for the Akan people, are given special names, such as "*Ababio* (has come again)…, *Akosan* (has gone and returned), *Ambewu* (you have not come only to die again)." Other names like *Kosama, Kaya*, and *Donkor*, for instance, will bear some facial or bodily cuts or markings. This is one way the Akan people identify the reincarnated.

But the larger question is: What other ways are the reincarnated identified? I cannot recall what my mother and I were talking about when she suddenly said to me that I am one of her dead twins reincarnated. I asked her how she knew that, but she laughed the matter off. When I persisted, she would only say that she knows every child of hers.

There are ways of ascertaining who has been reincarnated. The first is by naming a child after an ancestor whose essential nature the child assumes. In other words, the spirit of the ancestor descends on the infant during the naming rite so that the infant is imbued with all the essential character attributes of the ancestor. It is expected that the infant will grow up, behave, and make choices that are indiscernible from the ancestor's. Consequently, if the child behaves in ways that are incompatible with the ancestor's, society invariably reminds the child about the ancestor. The idea is that of conformity and so the child grows up exactly as society expects, in the image of the ancestor. After all, the spirit of the ancestor is expressed as genetic characteristic attributes in the child, and as spirit the child is protected by the stronger and omnipresent spirit of the ancestor.

Secondly, the most compelling evidence for identifying reincarnated children is the markings or cuts left on babies when they die. Cuts are deliberately inflicted on babies so that they can be identified upon their return from the spiritual world. Many parents have shown me such markings on their children as evidence of their once deceased children. They point to what appears to be sealed or closed holes on the ears of their male children as evidence that these boys in their previous existence were girls whose ears were pierced soon after birth.

An elderly woman told me that her ten-year-old boy fell and broke his leg and died soon after. When she had her next child (a girl), she limped on the same left leg and complained of constant pains on the exact place where her son broke his leg. The girl, now in her late twenties, is no longer limping but occasionally experiences localized pains in her left leg.

Thirdly, the reincarnated is able to identify certain artifacts that previously belonged to him or her. This goes back to why one is reincarnated in the first place. That is, what its spiritual mother mandated or what the individual himself or herself willed before they died.

But do the reincarnated themselves know about their past existence? Insofar as society reinforces in them the belief to that effect some are conscious of their previous existence. But my discussants insist that many of the reincarnated in their adult life remain unconscious of their previous existence until certain rites, events, and actions trigger memories of their past lives. Sometimes one may find himself or herself at a location or involved in a venture for the first time and intuitively feel as if they have been there before. This experience is quite enigmatic, often causing pain and anxiety engendered by the elusiveness of the experience.

The soul is an indispensable part of this phenomenon. It is the bearer of the purpose of being, making it cognizant of what the individual must accomplish in the world. If an individual's life is terminated prematurely, the soul returns to God while the spirit goes to the paternal household and awaits reincarnation. It the spirit that is reincarnated, not the spiritual personality that becomes an ancestor.

Secondly, through the process of divination the nature and purpose of the soul can be deciphered. Divination may be performed whenever a person has reason to believe that one has lost touch with oneself, resulting in a series of misfortunes or unexplained circumstances. The appropriate clergy are consulted during which time the soul is telepathically consulted. Restoration to holistic life is, however, contingent upon the individual leading an ideal life as may be mandated by one's soul. But while the soul remembers the individual's previous existence, the fact that the person is in a new body makes it difficult to determine precisely the individual's previous existence until certain rites have been performed.

And, finally, the phenomenon of reincarnation is a mystery, not meant to be known even by the reincarnated, except when one is highly developed or told about it by adepts. This is why in some cultures people are reincarnated into lesser creatures for as long as three thousand years before finally being reincarnated into human beings. However, this is not so in many African cultures, including the Akan, where people are always reincarnated as human beings. But the secrecy about the phenomenon remains. For instance, if a person was born male he would be reincarnated female. Or, he will be born a male but to distant relatives or even wait until several generations later to be born.

But if the human being is a spiritual being and has an ideal domicile in the ancestral world, then why will it decide to live in a less than ideal milieu? We must understand that ethical existence and generativity is practiced in the mundane and not at Samanadze. In fact the only way to become a spiritual personality is to be a human being first since one cannot achieve ancestorhood until the person has been born, lived, died, and resurrected as a spiritual personality. The world then is the testing ground for ethical existence and generativity, the sole criterion for judgement in the ancestral world. What will a spirit be without first manifesting itself among the living? It will have no name and could not be invoked by the living for any reason or purpose because it does not exist.

As for the process of coming to life, I begin with pregnancy. The pregnancy experience itself is such that it calls for certain idiosyncrasies and rites that are adhered to strictly. Pregnancy is sacred and mysterious, a state that must be concealed as long as possible. Even when discovered, it is still a taboo to make direct reference to it or inquire about it from the expectant woman. Pregnancy is self-evident and to inquire about it is perceived by society as sinister. Accentuated by precariousness, anxiety, and danger, the expectant mother must be protected in every way possible from societal view. Furthermore, the secrecy surrounding pregnancy means that no one is allowed to offer gifts to the expectant mother. In fact, it is a taboo to offer gifts. To do so is perceived as malicious, perhaps wishing for miscarriage or for the fetus to have some defects.

I recall an incident in Liberia when my wife was pregnant with our first child. An acquaintance of ours gave us some gifts saying that he may not be available when my wife delivered so we should accept his gifts beforehand. We accepted the gifts, but disposed of them immediately. The disposal had nothing to do with superstition as it was our adherence to tradition. Moreover, since the man was an Akan and ought to have known better, we had no choice but to discard those gifts no matter how good his intentions might have been.

To accept gifts can exacerbate the state of anxiety. What if the fetus is aborted? The Akan protocol mandates that the individual only welcomes a stranger when that person has arrived safely. In light of the clairvoyance of infants and the belief in reincarnation, the fetus is believed to be embarking on a journey from the ancestral world fully conscious of what is happening in the mundane world, and to present it with gifts before it arrived (born) may cause it to return (die) to where it originated. Perhaps the fetus may have been sent by its spiritual mother for exactly the same purpose: to return with as much wealth as possible. In fact, not until the eighth day do the Akan regard the neonate as a living being; it is still counted among the spiritual personalities.

These practices, merely the gist of the numerous taboos and prohibitions associated with pregnancy, are not necessarily attributable to the high infant mortality rate. Every society has its way of dealing with the of question death, and one way the Akan come to terms with death is through spirituality. The fact is, in spite of the remarkable scientific innovations that have certainly reduced infant deaths, scientists are still puzzled by the sudden infant death syndrome. Could such deaths have theological underpinnings, as the Akan people recognize? Is any death free of some form of similar interpretation?

Conception begins when the woman misses her menses. This calls for the observation of certain rites within the privacy and tutelage of the husband's paternal deity.[8] Although adherence to some of the strict prenatal rites are now hardly observed, some are still followed. Even in cases where the unmarried teenager is found to be pregnant, family members place her under the care of a doctor. Consequently, the expectant woman comes under the care of the doctor throughout gestation and parturition. These doctors, known notoriously in the West as witch doctors, know the family and medical histories of all their patients in their repertoire of oral knowledge. And so whenever a child falls ill, the parent's immediate reaction is to call for their traditional family practitioner.

When I was studying the different herbs, roots, tree barks, and intrapartal care, I asked the midwife precisely when the expectant mother begins with her treatments. She said:

> As soon as the woman realizes that she is pregnant, that is, when she misses her menstrual cycle then you start with these…herbs to help the baby grow strong in the hope of preventing miscarriages. This may continue until birth. Sometimes the baby may not show any sign of life, and for fear that the child may be born unhealthy the woman begins taking these …herbs and barks two or three time a week as enemas, changing medication weekly or bi-weekly or even monthly throughout pregnancy. These make the baby strong while those…make the mother healthy and strong. New medicines are introduced every trimester until birth, and there are some meant to ward off evil but that is mostly the job of the doctor. I try also to warn them from certain diets and herbs, such as…because they can induce abortion just like that.[9]

The treatments received by expectant mothers fall under three main classifications. First, the bulk of these medicines are administered as enema. This form of application is extremely crucial during the first trimester of pregnancy. One reason is that some women may continue to observe intermittent flow of menstrual blood during the initial stages of pregnancy, which may lead to the illusion of normalcy of menstruation. To end the intermittent flow of blood enemas are prescribed to effect cessation of the issue of blood and strengthen the pregnancy. The regularity of the enemas is contingent upon the state of pregnancy. The concoction and dosage vary according to each pregnancy and duration and stage of gestation. In most cases the enemas are administered during the early part of the day and evening. Afternoon enemas are discouraged because of the intensity of afternoon heat.

Secondly, the medicinal prescriptions are meant to ensure the well-being of the expectant mother. The very experience of pregnancy for some women, especially if this is their first pregnancy, makes them ill. The health of an expectant mother commands the utmost concern of her loved ones and so she is offered different kinds of medicines, which she must use under the watchful supervision of her family. These medications are taken by mouth whenever necessary or applied locally to areas considered a source of potential danger to her.

Thirdly, and most importantly, most of the medicines are subsumed under prophylactics. Society is acutely aware of and obsessed with the supernatural, particularly evil powers that seek to destroy anything that has the potential for good. And expectant mothers are prime targets for such malign forces. This is the single most important reason why pregnancies are kept secret until they become self-evident, when it is too late for any malicious person to cause any potential harm. Unless such steps are taken, it is believed that someone with an evil eye (*enyiwa bon*) may cause harm to the fetus and result in a stillbirth. Moreover, it is believed witches during their nocturnal escapades can actually remove the fetus from the womb of the sleeping mother, turning the fetus into whatever object or animal they choose. The sickly fetus will be returned at the end of their escapades, just before the mother wakes up.

To protect against such an event, different prophylactics are prescribed for the expectant mother. The medicines are put in water solution for the expectant woman to bathe in at designated times. Initially, she may make the trips to the doctor's home to bathe but may later bring home some medicines and prepare the solution for her intermittent baths.

Sometimes inoculative measures are taken by marking different parts of the expectant mother's body, such as the joints. Various concoctions are fried until charred, then grounded into powdered form and introduced directly into the markings which may be oozing with blood. The charred powder may also be licked or transformed into a talisman and given to her to wear around her waist. But even here the woman is always on guard against anyone who might unwittingly say or do anything that might be perceived as malicious.

Beside treatments requiring some sort of specialist, there are many socially accepted norms of behavior the couple is encouraged to follow. For instance, the couple is encouraged to copulate during gestation. The father being the conduit of spirit protects the mother and the fetus spiritually from any harm or danger. To underscore the protective nature of the paternal spirit the sleeping arrangement of the Akan is such that the male always sleeps in front of the female. The sleeping position must be such that if the woman has to get up she may have to go over or around her husband. What is meant here is that the man not only protects the woman spiritually but physically as well. In times of danger the man is the first to rise up to confront whatever the perceived danger or threat is. He must have unimpeded access to the door to arrest the threat, and by the same token be the first to be attacked.

This protective spiritual role is not exclusively male, however. There are instances when mothers of unmarried pregnant girls play the same role as men do. That is, the girls come under the tutelage of their mothers' paternal spirit. Most of the women who assume the role of "men" are post-menopausal women, who for all practical purposes, have become men. These women are in better positions to offer prenatal advice to the expectant mothers.

The pregnant woman's stomach is believed to be high during gestation, consequently when the stomach begins to drop anxiety sets in. This way of characterizing the expectant woman serves to confirm the notion that the unborn child is descending from the ancestral world believed to be in the sky. Some pregnant women may move in with their doctor or midwife, or the midwife's visits to the pregnant woman's house become frequent. The woman is told to curtail her daily chores, as most pregnant women continue to work until about their due date.

When the woman experiences contraction, the midwife is immediately called. Upon her arrival she puts her hands underneath the woman's armpits from behind and caresses her stomach. When labor commences and after all precautionary measures have been taken, the midwife then proceeds to tell the woman to push. If all goes well, the baby follows. Immediately after birth the neonate must cry. If not, it is given sharp slaps to the buttocks, prompting it to utter its first words. As soon as it cries, a sigh of relief comes over all those present. They now know that the first critical phase has passed and that the baby will survive. The umbilical cord is tied and cut, but the mother is not out of danger yet. She must expel the placenta, which in most cases occurs without any complications. When the expulsion takes longer than usual the midwife may give the mother some concoction to facilitate expulsion, or the mother may be rushed to the hospital. There have been many fatalities during this transitional period, exacerbated by logistical problems in getting women to hospitals. When such fatalities do occur, blame is passed around as to whether or not parturition should have occurred at the house in the first place. In this respect one has to take into consideration the psychological and spiritual concerns of the Akan people, to even begin to understand their reluctance to seek hospital care when sick.

The expelled placenta is buried at the house where the delivery occurred. The interred placenta serves as an anchorage for the neonate throughout life; that is, the individual is communally grounded and is expected to always find the way home. The individual's matrikin folks will always receive him or her. Thus the individual is never alone and without a home.

Similar treatment is given to the two inches or so of naval cord that drops off of the neonate after a few days. The mother keeps the cord in the infant's cosmetics tray where it stays until lost. Or, a fisherman, for instance, may use it as bait when he goes fishing or simply drops it into the sea. A mother may take it with her into a stream and with the infant on her back or side and offer prayers of success for the infant and then drops it into a stream.

Subsequently, people who wander are often asked whether or not their cords are missing, or if their placentas were not given the proper ritual treatment (burial). In the same way the placenta ties the fetus to its mother, the buried placenta symbolizes the relationship between the individual and mother earth, Asase Efua. Birth, therefore, does not sever the mother-child rapport because the child is made up of its mother's blood.

Post-partum care commences immediately following birth and continues for about three months. The mother's intrauterine therapy begins with the "sitting on hot water" at least twice daily for the first few weeks and whenever necessary in subsequent weeks. When a woman has twins the duration of this treatment is extended as long as necessary. While she sits on hot water (actually she sits on a stool while the water is placed before her open legs) she is covered with (except head) layers of cloth to prevent the steam from escaping. She then stirs the water with a stick until the steam is exhausted. The steam is believed to be curative and heals every intrauterine wound. This steam therapy, coupled with enemas and other herbal intakes combine to restore wholeness to the mother within three months of giving birth.

During gestation the expectant woman is expected to put on colored, old but clean cloth to reflect the danger, struggle, and anxious state of gestation. Upon parturition new, predominantly white clothes, beads, and myrrh are put on to signify victory. This continues for the first trimester after birth. At the onset of the second trimester she is considered healthy and so her clothes undergo another change commensurate with that period. Having already begun to carry the baby, she now is allowed to put on colorful clothes and jewelry, and allowed to carry her baby on her back anywhere she chooses.

Notes

1. Ephirim-Donkor, *African Personality and Spirituality: The Akanfo Quest for Perfection and Immortality*, (Ann Arbor, Michigan, 1994), pp. 34-35.
2. *Fufu* is prepared by pounding cooked yam or cassava and plantain with a pestle in a mortar until the ingredients coalesce into a sticky mass which is eaten with soup.
3. Ephirim-Donkor, *African Personality and Spirituality*, p.39.
4. It must be noted that the Akan people have seven *ebusua* or blood linear groups that form the basis for their matrilineal system of descent, traceable to a common primordial woman.
5. Antubam, op. cit., pp.90-93.
6. Ibid.
7. Ibid.
8. Christensen, *Double Descent Among the Fanti*, pp. 82-83.
9. Ephirim-Donkor, *African Personality and Spirituality*, p. 96.

CHAPTER 4

MY FATHER AND I ARE ONE

The Sunsum

In cases involving custody of children the Akan people would often times say to the matrikin that the father is the progenitor. Although the Akan understand gestation and parturition to be exclusively a female phenomenon, both sexes make such contradictory claims attributing childbirth to the father, literally. The source of the literal paradox is figurative or spiritual. The father imparts life unto his offspring, giving all spiritual, psychological, and characteristic attributes.

It is believed that all children are born because of their fathers, and children who do not come under the aegis of their fathers may die, be taken ill, or simply lead a delinquent life. So while parturition is biologically impossible for fathers, their inalienable spiritual rights are affirmed in the lives of their offspring.

The father exercises spiritual and psychological control over his offspring throughout their lives, reflected in the beginning by his right to name on the eighth day or thereafter. To say that the father is the progenitor is to accept the double foci the statement carries, that is, that the father imparts as well as takes away life. A father's anger ends in the death of his child by depriving it of spiritual identity or force. Vulnerable, the child succumbs to attacks by malign forces. An angry father thus need not speak, his silence brings the threat of doom. It is important therefore to maintain a good rapport with one's patrikin to ensure spiritual tutelage and blessings.

A child whose father denied fathering it might die or may grow up angry because he or she does not have any spiritual anchor. I really don't know what would happen to sperm-bank children born to women nowadays. Such a thought is inconceivable in Akan society because of the way society is structured, where an individual is required to involve one's patrikin and matrikin during the performance of certain rites, such as marriage and funeral. But who knows, in a rapidly changing world perhaps there may come a time when society would make room for such exigencies. Moreover, in the context of the *ebusua*, sperm-bank children would be considered full citizens.

To fill any potential spiritual vacuum a fatherless child might have, a father figure is sought to fill the void left by the biological father. The mother's brothers, father, or other male relatives assume the father's role during the capriciously vulnerable infancy period.

The basis for paternal influence in relation to maternal properties is expressed most strongly in what the Akan people call the *sunsum*. The *sunsum* is interpreted as something unseen or invisible. Hence *sunsum* is spirit. Yet it manifests itself psychologically as characteristics in every person. It is the father's spirit or *sunsum* that activates the mother's blood. The *sunsum* is an intrinsic quality that manifests itself in outward traits of individual temperament.

Still the *sunsum* can exist independently of human beings, having a spiritual being of its own. For instance, the spirits (*asunsum*) of the deities have power beyond and above that of humans. These deities intermittently manifest themselves through spirit possession. These spirits alight on the heads of their devotees during religious ceremonies, emitting responses from the audience like: "The individual has been possessed." When that happens the entire disposition of the possessed changes as she or he begins to sway from side to side, rising up and pacing back and forth. The possessed may begin to undress themselves, if they are members of the clergy. In this situation, another member of the clergy rises up and starts striking a gong or ringing a bell. The possessed will follow the one making the sounds toward a room where she or he will be attired in ceremonial costume to begin her public display.

Other events of spirit possession take place during festivals for twins. For the Akan and the Guan community of Winneba, a complete set of twins must be made up of five children. These are the twins, Panyne and Kakra, followed by three more births, namely, Tawiah, Abam, and Nyankomagow. As Tawiah myself I have not only gone through some of these rites, but have observed in the town of Winneba twins festivals during which the twin deity, Abam Kofi, possessed many of the participants.

The essential nature of the *sunsum*, whether as an intrinsic entity or an extrinsic agent of some sort possessing a subject, is that it has to do with disposition. That is, it alters one's character attributes or ego. The individual is brought under the dictate and influence of the spirit through internal and external means. The *sunsum* is experienced tangibly through human actions, no matter how unconventional those actions might be.

Yet another reason for defining *sunsum* as spirit is based on the distinction made between physical things (*honam mu*) and spiritual things (*sunsum mu*). For instance, a disease can have a spiritual source (*sunsum mu yar ba*), in which case no medical (physical) treatment will suffice. Holistic healing is sought instead from clergy who are believed to communicate telepathically with the causative malign spirits.[1]

When told that my older sister had been taken ill, I requested that she get medical treatment immediately. Yet when I telephoned Ghana about her prognosis I was told that her illness was spiritual in nature and would not require hospitalization. When at last I was able to get to Ghana and saw her, I was moved to tears. Only miraculous intervention could save her; She died several hours later. I am still angry as I write because my sister would have lived if she had been taken to the hospital. But the supernatural presupposition of my relatives was such that no amount of telephone calls could sway them toward treatments other than the spiritual.

What has precipitated this trend is the emphasis Western health care-givers put on curing only the body. At best it is psychosomatic. But

even here there is a difference between the way the Western community deals with mental disorders and the way traditional health care-
givers go about their business. If the medical community does not
address the spiritual source of illnesses, then how can they treat them?
While the Western community puts emphasis on curing the body, the
traditional health care-givers stress healing.

In this and other ways the Akan people believe that the *sunsum*
makes its presence known in the physical. It manifests itself by taking
hold of the material and transforming characteristic attributes. In a possession or joining, the nature of the *sunsum* can be explained in the
analogous act of sexual love, where the physical is wedded to the spiritual. Many of the clergy are married to their deities in this way. The
entire process of spirit possession, a *call*, and being a novitiate (*akom-
fa*) represent this type of relationship.

To be called into the clerical vocation is to be possessed by the
spirit of the divinity that called the priest. Moreover, the clergy must
perceive that divinity in order for him or her to be in conversation with
it. But most importantly, the clergyperson must know the name of the
deity that called him or her. This is what being a novice entails, and
by the time the student graduates, it is expected that he or she has been
inculcated in all the mysteries of the order.

Nowadays we have many people pursuing clerical vocations without any sense of the spiritual. For these people the ministry is only a
job. I recall when I was studying for the Christian ministry, we were
asked to discuss our sense of the holy and spirituality in relation to our
calling. To my surprise, most of the students would not use the word
"Call" to refer to their religious experiences in relation to their clerical
vocation. While I respected their points of view, I come from a culture
where such a view would have been inconceivable.

At times during the practice of priestly functions, the union
between the possessed or matter and spirit result in divine conception,
and children born from such flirtation are called *abosom mba* (divine
children). These children may have dual properties of being divine
and human.

How do we explain this phenomenon? A childless couple or those
who lose their children at childbirth may make vows to a deity in
exchange for a conception or for their children to survive at birth. If
children are born after such a consultation, they are taken back and

dedicated along with other gifts to the deity as a way of honoring the original vow. The children are placed under the tutelage of the deity. As a sign of their divine births, the hair of the children may not be cut or kempt for the rest of their lives.

The important thing to remember is that such children are not considered to be the children of the biological parents but rather children of the deities. These children and their descendants are eligible for any clerical vocation. In other words, the deities only "call" their own children. And so not everyone is eligible for a clerical vocation, but only those born into royal and priestly families, twins and their descendants, and nazirites and their descendants.

In the 1970s the Ghanaian dailies ran stories about a group of African Americans who were in Ghana to pursue a clerical vocation. But the uniqueness of the story has to do with the trans-phenomenal nature of the calling. I was a teenager then, but I recall reading about the deity in Late called Akonede possessing these African Americans. The deity claimed that they were the descendants of her children who were taken into slavery and had gone to the United States to "call" them. Consequently, they were brought to Ghana to study under the priestess of the deity Akonede.

The Su and the Suban

The *sunsum* is incarnate in the infant as the *su* or essential nature. The su is qualitatively good, but has the potential for evil in manifestations later on in life. From the *su* the child develops the *suban*, the intrinsic character strengths and weaknesses genetically transmitted by the father for continuity. The *suban* has dual proclivities, *suban pa* (good natured) and *suban bon* (evil natured). As one matures, the individual's attitudes relationally determine a person's *suban*.

The *suban* is the intention behind outward expression. A person is said to have *suban pa* when exhibiting grace, obedience and respect for the elders, gratitude, and gregariousness. *Suban pa* results in acts that are meant to benefit society. The ethereal side of *suban pa* is glory that is thought to blaze and emanate from the face of the individual.

To use words like grace and glory conjures up God's qualities and, yes, that is the intention. God *is* "grace in the air" (*adom wo wim*) and to exhibit *suban pa* is to emulate God. The expression of *suban* is individual in nature but communal in its lasting effects. The Akan people are remembered long after they are dead according to the kind of *suban* they exhibited when they were alive. For the Akan this remembrance is not a nostalgic pastime but an active awareness that *suban pa* may be revisited upon the deceased's families. Thus the development of individual *suban* is central to the well-being of the family and to the Akan sense of community.

Nurturing of the formation of *suban* begins in infancy and continues through the educational period of maturation. The child is always corrected, quite often spanked when it does something wrong. When I fought with other boys, my grandmother would say to me: "I don't like that behavior" or "My character is not good." The point here is that children are born good, but during the developmental processes they acquire certain behavioral patterns deemed bad. Bad behavior must be eschewed by societal inculcation of the good.

The Wer and the Awerekyekyer

Another attribute of the *sunsum* is called *wer*, one's inherent will power or energy. The *wer* is inexhaustible energy associated closely with the heart and soul. It enables a person to face incredible odds with courage and resilience. Its quality is thus measured in terms of strength or weakness. One is said to have a strong will power when in the face of physical pain the individual is still able to cling to life tenaciously. Its influence, in fact, pervades throughout the living world. However, it is also understood that excessive display of the inherent will power or energy can be violent, even dangerous if not sublimated. This means that there is a violent side to every human being, the recognition of which leads to the cultivation of discretion, patience, and control.

An important attribute of the *wer* is that it is subject to the emotional fluctuations associated with the heart and the soul. The *wer* of a person is said to be low when experiencing grief and dejection (*no wer ahow*). The elevation of the *wer* is tantamount to the happiness of the soul and the heart. Therefore, the individual, or rather the wer, must maintain a balanced energy level necessary for healthy life.

There is a more benign, comforting side to the *wer* called *awerekyekyer*. For the Akan, to show *awerekyekyer* is to be human. Every person is believed to be endowed with a gentle, counselling, comforting spirit needed to alleviate the state of melancholia. Etymologically, the term is a conjugation of *wer* and *Kyekyer*, that is, to bind up or tie together. Thus anyone who binds the broken-hearted or consoles the needy is exhibiting this intrinsic quality aimed at restoring wholeness and bliss to the person.

The Ayamhyehye, the Ahummobor, and the Abadai

Actually to show *awerekyekyer*, the individual must have gone through three steps. The first is *ayemhyehye*, described as a burning, churning, or gnawing sensation within the stomach. This feeling is produced when one is confronted with human suffering engendered by deprivation and desolation, such as the pernicious devastation of war or a disaster. If one cannot move beyond this state, *ayemhyehye* becomes simply an apathetic state. Many people, especially women, are able to move beyond this state to a higher level called *ahummobor* (compassion).

When a person comes in contact with a dying or hungry person, his or her first intrinsic reaction is *ayemhyehye*. Naturally, most people would stop to help or alleviate the situation, but occasionally some would be inclined to move on without offering assistance (like the priest and the Levite in the Good Samaritan parable found in Luke 10:30-35). In the parable the priest and the Levite, representing the clergy, moved on when they came across a man beaten by thieves and left to die. Perhaps as clergy they were simply following the duties of their office by not coming in contact with a corpse. But whatever their reason, they did not move beyond *ayamhyehye*. However, if they had attended to the wounded man they would have shown *ahummobor* and demonstrated what it means to be human.

But one must also transcend *ahummobor* if the situation is to be arrested, otherwise, like *ayamhyehye*, *ahummobor* is just another apathetic state. The individual must exhibit *abadai* (beneficence). The beneficence of *abadai* relieves the state of want. It is only when these intrinsic qualities have been demonstrated that one can commence with *awerekyekyer*, that is, to actually tend the state of want. The Good Samaritan, unlike the priest and the Levite, experienced all four stages by being moved first to *ayamhyehye* when he saw the dying man. Then he had compassion or *ahummobor*, and he was propelled to act by alleviating the suffering of the dying man by showing *abadai*. While most people may stop at *abadai* by their altruism or philanthropy, *awerekyekyer* is a step beyond *abadai* in that it actually entails personally getting involved in the caring for and attending to a need.

These intrinsic attributes, though masculine, are feminine in their outward manifestations. Hence, to the Akan people Nana Nyame is the ultimate beneficent mother, the only one who epitomizes all these essential qualities towards God's children. So anyone who consciously demonstrates these qualities is being Godlike, and there are people like that who are assiduously trying to make a difference in the lot of humanity. But there are even more people out there who really don't care one way or another. Yet, there are those who are always being God-like but are not aware of these stages or steps.

The Sunsum (Shadow)

In addition to the cathectic and psychological qualities already discussed, the *sunsum* in its spiritual sense is manifested for the Akan people in the figure of the shadow. As individuals we perhaps notice our shadows for the first time as children. It is a shade in the form of the self, endowed with motion, mimicking our every act. The shadow might be described in its more mysterious aspect as something that is seen yet intangible.

To the Akan people this dark shape also is called *sunsum*. Its form during the day is merely an indication of its greater spiritual significance. For the *sunsum* has an existence independent of the individual, free of the confines of light. That is, it takes darkness to illuminate the precise nature of the *sunsum*. Just as there is a world of tangibility and objectivity characterized by light and sight, there is the metaphysical realm of subjectivity characterized by darkness, secrecy, and the mysterious. The corporeal world is governed by human beings; the incorporeal realm is under the domain of spiritual beings as evidenced by the dream world of shadows.

The images seen in the world of dreams are all shadows that continue the activities of the corporeal world beforehand. When human activity ceases during sleep, the *sunsum* of the sleeping person continues its chores in the realm of the sacred, activities that are a prelude to the course of events in the world of objectivity. Thus, dreams are

prophetic and predictive about future events, such as the next morning, even days, months, or years ahead. In other words, what is conceived in darkness is brought to actuality in the light because dreams
are a window to future eventualities. The images and characters seen
in the dream world are the same in the real world, or at least they will
become so. One literally sees him/herself in dreams, and there is no reason to assume otherwise symbolically or figuratively. So while the physical body sleeps, the *sunsum*'s activity in the metaphysical realm of
darkness illuminates, ironically, what would otherwise remain shrouded in mystery. In what way, then, does the individual decipher the
dream world? Concerning dream interpretation, Rattray writes:

> I shall give presently some examples of typical Ashanti dreams col-
> lected at random from the dream experiences of various individuals.
> From these it will be seen that, among the many varieties of dreams,
> certain dreams have received stereotyped explanations which are
> commonly accepted. It will be noted moreover that, broadly speak-
> ing, 'dreams go by contraries'."[2]

To base dream interpretations on contraries or the principle of oppo-
sites is dogmatic, and does not take into account the literary and symbolic representations that may hold the key to deciphering dreams. To
see the shadow as a dark shade in the light does not mean the *sunsum*
is dark. When perceived in the dream world it certainly does not appear
dark but as a living entity engaged in "normal" activities in the fluid
and fantastic world of dreams. To dream about money does not mean
impecunious the coming morning, days, or years; or to dream about
the death of someone does not mean longevity for the person. This
would have been the case if the law of contraries were true to dream
interpretations. In fairness, however, Rattray's interpretive fault lay not
in theory (that theory being an accepted approach in Western scholarship) but in application here.

There is a more critical and even frightening side to dreams insofar as the individual is concerned. Dreams are as distinct as the night
is from the day, and as real as the fear and apprehension an individual
may experience at night. If a dream proves to be profoundly disturbing, the individual invariably seeks help from the clergy. As instru-
ments of the deities, the clergy are able to make known through
divination what was otherwise unclear to the dreamer. If the dream is

malign, prophylactic rites are also enacted to ward off its realization.

Based on dreams I have analyzed since 1982, including my own, it would be wrong to interpret dreams utilizing the principle of contraries or wish-fulfillment alone. People react anxiously to their dreams because they are fearful of their potential ominous repercussions. Particularly, any dream interpretation that fails to consider the ethos of the Akan cannot be taken seriously.

I offer here one of my own dreams as a case in point. I had this dream in May, 1982, about four months after I arrived in West Virginia from Liberia:

> I was standing in front of my father's house facing the main highway that runs through my town. Suddenly I saw my daughter knocked down and killed by a car. I picked her up in my arms and said to her 'come back to life even if you are dead.' When I looked across the street I saw a woman whom I hated standing there and watching the whole incident passively.

I woke up sweating. When I checked the time it was three o'clock in the morning. I sat on my bed scared, not knowing what to do. Finally, I decided to make a telephone call to my wife who had flown with our daughter to Ghana from Liberia when I flew to the United States. I recounted the dream to her and asked her to take good care of our daughter.

Now it seems obvious why I reacted the way I did. My first inclination was to react by telling my wife because I took the dream literally, and by reacting the way I did my hope was to ward off any possible evil from happening. To my grief, about a month or so after this dream, I received a letter from a relative that my daughter had died suddenly. No, I thought, this could not be true. I read the letter several times as if I had misread it each time before. I was in the state of denial, unable to move beyond the shock of this news and unwilling to accept the truth. I was devastated.

But what was the dream saying to me? The intersection in which I was standing in the dream was a notorious spot. In my recollection, at least half a dozen people, including school children, have been killed there by automobiles. In the extent of the dream, the road represented ethical existence and death, for my daughter's life ended before she had the chance to live ethically. To be killed suddenly by a car meant that she would die a sudden, violent death. In fact, she dehydrated and died within twenty four hours or so. When I picked my daughter up in the dream and asked her to return to life I was simply reaffirming my belief in reincarnation, especially since she did not have the chance to begin her ethical life. The woman at the other side of the road was the culprit: the evil one, the witch, grandparent, doctor, prophet, priest, and the elder who is always blamed for all mishaps among the Akan people. Indeed, I blamed someone.

Several weeks after her death I dreamt about her again, but this time the dream transpired in Bluefield, West Virginia.

> I saw her ascending and descending a ladder at the house where I was staying. Finally, she stayed atop the ladder playing. I pursued her there but just as I was about to hold her she smiled and disappeared.

Since this dream in 1982 I have not dreamt about her again. The single most important archetypal symbol in the dream is the ladder. The Akan people believe that there is a death ladder, *owu atwer*, that must be ascended before entering the ancestral world. It takes forty days for the spiritual personality of the deceased to depart the corporeal to the world of the ancestors. So even though my dream transpired in another cultural milieu, the symbolism and content remained the same. That is, the dream must be perceived in the context of post-forty day farewell apparition by my daughter.

The literal meanings of dreams are such that often relationships are strained because characters of relatives were villainously perceived in dreams. Despite the fact that these characters are the shadows of relatives or siblings, they serve to depict their unconscious or ulterior motives. It is only a matter of time before they manifest themselves to the dreamer. Although it may seem absurd to others, it would be unwise to take lightly dreams in which characters are perceived as antagonists or witches. It can lead to irreconcilable sibling differences.

The Ntoro/Egyabosom

Alongside the seven uterine blood groups, the *ebusua*, are twelve loosely organized agnatic groups called *ntoro*. The precise nature of the *ntoro* groups has been put forward by J. H. Nketia.[3] The *ntoro*, Nketia explains, are "groups of people compounded of the same spiritual essence, distinguished from one another by the river they wash in and by the details of religious observances, rites and prohibitions, by the creatures they venerate and by the greeting response that they expect to be used in reply to their greetings."[4]

From Nketia it is quite clear that the *ntoro* is a kind of cultic, esoteric, spiritually oriented group, bound together by idiosyncratic rituals. The following are the twelve *ntoro-egyabosom* groups and their characteristic attributes: *bosompra*/the tough; *bosomtwi*/the human; *bosommuru*/the distinguished; *bosom-nketea* or *bosompo*/the audacious; *bosom-dwerebe*/the eccentric; *bosom-akom*/the fanatic; *bosomafi*/the chaste; *bosomayesu*/the truculent; *bosom-konsi*/the virtuoso; *bosomsika*/the fastidious; *bosomafram*/the liberal; *bosomkrete*/the chivalrous.[5]

Conspicuous about each *ntoro* group is the prefix *bosom*. But unlike the moon (*Bosom*), *bosom* here means a deity or divinity. The question is why would the moon and the divinities share the same term? The divinities are the first spiritual children of God who traverse the universe at the behest of God. On earth they are associated with elements, objects, and bodies of water or rivers. That is, these elements or objects serve as mediums of manifestation for the deities.

Thus the suffixes represent mostly rivers or bodies of water and elements that are sacred to those who share the same *ntoro* as the deities. Moreover, each *ntoro* has its own sacred day. What constitute the *ntoro* are the collective spirits of the departed patrikin folks. These spirits, rather than travel to the ancestral world, remain in the paternal household to provide protection for the living members while awaiting reincarnation.

I used to ask my African American students what Greek fraternities have to do with them. My reason was to draw their attention to the fact that Africans and particularly the Akan, also have fraternal orders that can best serve them in their quest for continuity and heritage. Most would respond by saying they didn't know about these African orders, while others simply didn't care one way or another.

The Osaman

We have already seen how the *sunsum* or spirit of a divinity traverses the cosmos and makes itself known by possessing a subject. Furthermore, it has been shown how the *sunsum* as an intrinsic entity is transmitted to the child via the father's semen. What concerns me here is the nature of the personality after death. The dead one has a transformed "personality" the Akan people call the 'saman. The osaman is an abstract personality, yet it is tangible enough to have a *sunsum* of its own. But no one would say that they have "seen" the *sunsum* of a deceased person, rather they would say that they have seen the *osaman* of the deceased. This confirms that the *osaman* is tangible.

Only under certain conditions might someone claim to have seen an *osaman*. The notion is that it takes forty days after death for the *osaman* to depart for the ancestral world. However, before the 'saman makes its final departure, it may materialize before some members of its family. I vividly recall my paternal grandmother waking up at dawn and wailing, saying my father had appeared to her. This was about one month after his death.

Stories about such apparitions are commonplace, and those who attest to such apparitions say that the *asaman* (plural) they encounter possess bodies like everyone else, appearing in only a matter of seconds. In general, the Akan hold that the *asaman* reveal themselves for many reasons, e.g., to show or tell them about hidden treasures, bid final farewell to or visit with other relatives who may not be aware of their deaths, and disappear before the relatives are told about their demise. For instance, an *osaman* may come and knock on the door of a loved one. Or, it may be heard engaging in a favorite activity, one the deceased person loved doing in life. Most of these apparitions occur at night before the fortieth day. The departure of the *osaman* means that it will not be seen again until its living relatives are faced with life-threatening illnesses or are going through crises. Then the *osaman* would appear in a dream to assure those relatives of its omnipresence in their ordeal, otherwise the *osaman* will not be seen at all.

Yet another phenomenon engendered by the lingering effect of the purpose of being causes an *osaman* to defer going to the ancestral world. This phenomenon happens to those whose deaths are felt to be premature and who are thought to have died without completing their ethical existence and generativity. Such *asaman* simply assume human form elsewhere, taking up an anonymous existence far from relatives to live out the remainder of their purpose of being (nkrabea). If per-chance they are discovered by an acquaintance, they vanish instanta-neously, leaving the assumed family ignorant of their true identities.

Once again the *asaman* simply move to another remote town and continue their existence.

It is believed that some of these spiritual personalities may actually marry and have families. I have been shown the children of one such union, but I have not made any attempt to ascertain from the children their identities. It is said that the children insisted on seeing their father's hometown and their grandparents until one day he agreed to take them. When they drew near, he sent the children and their mother ahead while he went on an errand. That was the last time he was seen. Stories like this abound in Akan culture, but the important thing to remember is that a spiritual personality has the ability to materialize, taking on human form and living as a human being. It takes the old and those with clairvoyance to recognize these *asaman* beings. Mostly, they are found in crowded places, and are thought to come out when it is raining and the sun is shining concurrently. They are said to speak from their nasals and emit certain unpleasant odors that are symptomatic of their metamorphic personalities.

The spiritual personality thus is none other than the once living person but in an abstract personality. The change of existence further suggests a belief in an after-life composed of spiritual beings of immortal natures. Once attaining this form of existence, the *osaman* must be judged by the ancestors on the merit of its life on earth after crossing a river and finally climbing a ladder to Samanadze. Life's quest is to achieve that ideal and bequeath to the ebusua a name worthy of evocation. Having been found worthy by the ancestors, the spiritual personality is endowed with immortality, omniscience, and ubiquity as an ancestor.

The Sasa

For the Akan people the nature and circumstance of death determines the nature of the spiritual personality, that is, whether the spiritual personality will ascend to the spiritual world or not. The fact is, not every one who dies goes to the ancestral world automatically. The question then is, Where do the spiritual personalities of those who are unable to ascend to the ancestral world go?

Abnormal and unusual deaths, such as suicides, drowning, accidents, death during pregnancy, and homicides are deemed evil and taboo. An individual who suffers such a death is referred to as *'tofo*, and his or her spiritual personality is known as a *sasa* rather than *osaman*. The *sasa* is an agitated spirit in limbo, without a final resting place. It can neither ascend into Samanadze nor take residence among humanity; consequently it keeps vigil at the place where the death occurred.

The very nature of such deaths make the *asasa* (plural) malign spirits, often terrorizing relatives in their dreams, especially if a death is unknown to the relatives. My discussants related many stories concerning encounters with asasa. The one common characteristic about them is that they are very hostile. For example, if the death occurred at a house, the sasa makes the house uninhabitable for anyone by virtue of its intermittent apparitions aimed at frightening away prospective tenants. The way people respond to this phenomenon is by performing exorcism in the house or on the spot where the *sasa* lingers.

The *sasa* may also be understood in the form of blood when dealing with homicides. The blood of a murdered person is said to have turned into a *sasa* in pursuit of the murderer for revenge. And until the murderer is brought to justice, the blood of the murdered rests not only on the murderer but his or her entire family. This may continue until the murderer confesses and the appropriate rites are performed to release the sasa into eternal bliss.

The Dzen

Perhaps the most important of the paternal components for the Akan people is the *dzen* or name. The name is the final seal of a complete person, without which the individual cannot exist. It is paramount therefore that a sacred day, place, and time be set for such a rite. Upon receiving his or her name, the individual is counted among the human family.

For the Akan people names are of extreme importance. After all, that is what existence is about: To lead a good life and achieve the most precious prize of all, an ideal name (*dzen pa*) for posterity. Therefore, in addition to adhering to social decorum needed for the formation of a strong social and ethical perspective, the child is "expected to emulate the character of the one whose name he takes."

The individual receives two names after the first eight days of his or her existence. The first is assumed automatically and unconditionally by virtue of being born alive on any given day. This name, known

as the person's "day name" (*da dzen*) or "soul name" (*kradzen*), is determined by the day of the week on which the child was born. To distinguish between the sexes the Akan have seven pairs of opposite soul-day
names after the days of the week. They believe that these names represent seven qualitative souls of God and have direct bearing on the
individual. These seven souls of God are: "*Asi, Adwo, Abena, Aku,
Awuo, Afi, Amen.*" In other words, the neonate is born with a God-soul,
based on the quality of God in attendance on that day. The names of
the weekdays are *Dwewda*/Monday, *Benada*/Tuesday, *Wukuda*/
Wednesday, *Yawoda*/Thursday, *Fida*/Friday, *Memenda*/Saturday, and
Kwesida/Sunday. These correspond with seven pairs of names assumed
by children, namely, Adjowa, Adwowa; Abena, Alaba, Araba; Akua,
Ekuwa; Yaa, Aba, Awo; Afua, Efua; Amma, Amba; and Esi, Asi, Akosua
for females. The male names are: Kojo, Kwadwo; Kobena, Kwabena,
Ebo; Kweku, Kwaku; Yaw, Ywaw, Kwaw, Kow; Kofi, Kwafi; Kwame,
Kwamena; Kwesi, Kwasi.

What is remarkable about these divine names and their corre-
sponding days are that they have their own characteristic attributes.
These intrinsic characteristics explain certain behavioral patterns and
why people do things in a certain way, although most people are oblivious to these intrinsic influences. Those born on Mondays are believed
to be quiet, peaceful, respectful, and supplicants (*okoto*).[6] They are intro-
verts. The Tuesday-born is said to be "obarema" or masculine, strong,
and extravert. But masculinity is balanced with a more feminine side,
that is, compassion (*ogyam*).[7] The Wednesday-born is known as *Eku sika*
(gold), that is, tenacious, wealthy, and as hard as a rock (sika). That is
to say: "'He buys and decides for you' concurrently. Consequently the
Wednesday born is said to be mean-spirited or 'dark hearted.'"[8]

To be born on Thursday is to be aggressive (*pirba, Preko*), courageous, eager to confront, fight, and engage.[9] The reverse side of their
nature is that they suffer from "ingratitude" since their aggressiveness
is often misconstrued. The recalcitrance and restlessness of the Friday-
born makes him or her an adventurer. One is always on the move, quite
often against the wishes of others. As for the Saturday-born, he or she
is thought to be sensational,[10] tendentiously precise (*atoapoma*), and is
often referred to as "Master of Serpent's Antidote" (*otanankaduro*).[11]
Their sensationalism is attributable to their wealth of knowledge, often
compelling the individual to act precipitously. Finally, to be born on

Sunday is to be *"obue-akwan,"* that is, to guide, to lead, and pave the way for others to follow. Thus, the Sunday-born is a leader. Appropriately enough, he or she is known as *"Bodua"* (whisk). A whisk is a symbol of power and authority. As a leader one is empowered to lead, guide, and protect with the whisk.

Often used interchangeably with the soul-day attributes are praise names (*nsabran, abodzen*). To get the best out of a person it may be expedient to utilize praise names to arouse or gratify the person, especially if they are engaged in altruistic causes or even in acts deemed beneath the individual. In order to quiet our infant son my wife often finds herself singing a lullaby using his praise name, *preko.*

The names and their inherent strengths and attributes ensure unity of the person with his or her soul. For this reason, it is the responsibility of the community of faith to observe all rites on behalf of the young. For these rites to attain their efficacy, however, they must be performed on the original time. For instance, a naming rite must be performed on the eighth day, when the soul of the infant is in attendance. Hence, to celebrate a birthday based solely on dates is profane and foreign because sacred time cannot be altered or compromised. On the eighth day or thereafter, the neonate acquires its formal name (*dzen pa*). This name too has its own idiosyncrasies that serve as a continuum for the ancestral world. After thoughtful deliberation by some members of the child's patrikin, a name is chosen based on the gender of the child and given on the eighth day or thereafter. The choice of names may follow a systematized formula. For example, a father should not name a child after his parents when his grandparents have not been named. To name one's parents first is considered disrespectful to the grandparents. The order of seniority must be followed. Furthermore, a father must name all of his patrilineage (*egya fie*) before naming his matrilineage (*na fie*). And since a father may not be old enough to know most of his patrikin folks, it is always wise for him to consult with his patrikin before naming his child.

The postnatal naming rite (*dzen to*) must commence and end before sunrise. The neonate may remain at the maternal household or be taken to the paternal household. Occasionally the matrikin will petition the neonate's patrikin for the right to name the child. The request may or may not be granted, since the right to name is exclusively paternal.

While the father names his own children, he will yield to older siblings or members of his paternal household who wish to perform the rite. At the many naming rites that I have attended I have yet to witness a biological father perform a naming rite. Any member of the patrikin can bestow the selected name upon the neonate. As Rattray explains, "the infant's own father, paternal grandfather, father's brother, father's brother's son, father's brother's daughter, father's sister, and so on"[12] have the honor of naming the child.

Occasionally a father's right to name is forfeited when he denies fathering a child, in which case the infant's matrikin bestows the name. However, if at some point he admits to fathering the child, then a heavy fine is levied against the father and his patrikin. If the father is able to pay the fine, then he reclaims his child but may not rename the child. During the naming rite two elements are used. Two cups, one containing water and the other liquor, are each placed on a table. An elder first invokes God and the ancestors by pouring a libation. The infant is next presented to the elder with its head resting on the elder's left elbow. Or, the infant is laid on the elder's lap, face-up. The elder announces the infant's name to the audience for the first time and then dips the index finger into the cup of water and touches the mouth of the infant with the accompanying words: "When you say it's water, then it is." The same ritual is repeated with the liquor: "When you say it's liquor, then it is." Some elders alternate between the elements, but either way it must be repeated three times.

What do these acts mean? The facial expressions of the infant unquestionably change, especially when it tastes the liquor. In some cases they may even cry. The infant may not see the elements to make visual discernment, but it is certainly aware of the difference between the water and the liquor when it tastes them. But that is precisely the point. The elements and its accompanying words mean that the neonate should be tenacious and let its *yea* be *yea* and its *nay* be *nay*. The infant is exhorted to be truthful, make the right choices in life, and stand by them no matter how painful (liquor) or pleasing (water) they may be. Just as water and liquor may appear the same but be dissimilar in taste, so it is with truth and falsehood sometimes. Therefore the infant should grow up and exercise mental acuity, especially during deliberation. Of course, the infant is expected to take after the one whose name it now bears, and the community of faith helps in that process by inculcating the infant to take after the ancestor.

The remainder of the water and liquor are mixed together and given to the parents to drink. In some communities the father will drink all but a portion which he will bend down and pour backwards between his legs as a sign of fecundity. Some of my discussants maintain that the drinking of the mixture by the mother marks the beginning of breast-feeding symbolically. Others contend that the ritual simply attests to the parental bond between infant and parents. The parents, they say, must share with their child the same food or element, that is, whatever is eaten by the child must also be good enough for its parents and vice versa.

At this point money may be introduced to the neonate. The elder holds a coin and speaks to the infant about the importance of money and how he or she must work hard to acquire wealth. The elder places the coin into the infant's palm and then puts it into a plate. At this juncture anyone who wishes to offer gifts proceeds to offer them. This is the first time during the naming rite that the community sees the infant and presents it with gifts.

The remainder of the liquor in the bottle is then shared with all present. The officiant moves from person to person and as he shares the liquor announces the name to the recipient, who drinks it to the health of the infant. This continues until everyone has partaken of the drink. If someone arrives late the ritual of sharing the drink is repeated.

In this way the father earns his spiritual rights over his offspring. The child first hears and responds to a specific sound that permeates its inner being. As the child grows it associates and identifies with its name long before it learns how to write it—or never learns how to write it at all, if it is born into an oral community.

He who names owns, thus the father owns and controls his offspring by naming and thus blessing them. Every person lives his or her name, that is, their destiny. And it doesn't really make any difference whether or not a person loves or hates his or her father. To have and actually know one's father is to be spiritually grounded and alive, otherwise one traverses the world aimlessly in search of one's spiritual kind, the father's. Without this spiritual bonding an individual is spiritually dead. This is why for the Akan people a child does not exist until named by a member of its patrikin on the eighth day or thereafter.

N o t e s

1. Field, *Search for Security* (London: Faber & Faber, 1960), p. 14.
2. Rattray, *Religion and Art in Ashanti*, p. 192.
3. See J. H. Nketia, *Funeral Dirges of the Akan* (Achimota, Ghana 1955).
4. Ibid., p. 26.
5. Busia, "The Ashanti" in Daryll Forde (ed.), *African Worlds*, p. 199.
6. Danquah, op. cit., p. 48.
7. Ibid.
8. Ibid.
9. Ibid.
10. Ibid.
11. Danquah, op. cit., p. 47.
12. Rattray, *Religion and Art in Ashanti*, p. 62.

C h a p t e r   5

THE DIVINE PRESENCE

One cannot speak about achieving divinity without first exploring the source and nature of the concept. Hence the question: Who then is Nana Nyame? Perhaps based on the creation myth, ethnographers conceived of the God as a "sky God," "Supreme being," or "High God."[1] However, the Akan name for God above does not transliterate as sky, high, or supreme. If, however, these appellations were conceived by associating Nana Nyame with the sky, then could not the same be said about the Gods of all religions and peoples? In fact, the sky (*osor*) or infinite heights (*wim*) make no reference to any name of God, neither do they make reference to God as sky, high, or supreme being, although God has appellations that describe God as supreme, powerful, and eternal. On the contrary, God, as divine, must be shielded from the dome of the sky above, and from the earth below, as depicted in the dialogue between God and the Old Woman. Similarly, the Akan king is shielded from the sky by a huge umbrella and from the earth by his or her *ahenmba* (royal) sandals. The king, then, is no more the sky than

God is: they are simply both divine.

Existentially, God is not glued to the sky, as if God could not descend to earth and involve itself in the life of the individual or the world. Existence is only by the grace (*adom*) of God. So when people enquire about the well-being of others or when they respond to greetings they respond by saying: "By God's grace, I am fine" (Nyame *adom*). To bid farewell to someone embarking on a journey, the usual address is: "Depart with God" (*nnye Nyame nko*). When consoling the bereaved one may say: "God exists" (*Nyame wo ho*); "Because of God, everything will be made right" (*Nyame ntsi, obeye yie*); "Put your trust in God" (*fa wo wer hye Nyame mu*); and "Leave it to God" (*fa ma Nyame*).

God's pervasiveness in Akan thought is such that God's ubiquity is often taken for granted. From sunrise to sundown the name of God is on the lips of people and, because of that, people respond with dismay when tragedies arise. Thereupon people begin to question and call upon God to protect, defend, and guide. But God is not thought to be the culprit, rather the individual or society is blameworthy due to unethical existence (*obra bon*), which calls for existential reexamination with the cosmos via rites to restore the right triadic balance.

God could not be responsible for the ills of society because God is love (*Nyame ye odo*), and under no circumstance would God remove God's love from humanity. The love of God is predicated upon the fact that God abhors evil (*Nyame mpe bon*). Therefore to lead an unethical life is to alienate oneself from God, resulting ultimately in death. Moreover, the righteousness of God is based on the fact that every injustice is duly recompensed (Nana Nyame *botua wo ka*). The concept of divine retribution is deeply imbedded in the Akan thought, as the individual who has suffered unjustly would invoke the divine curse: "God will recompense." Paradoxically, God is death, as expressed in these riddles: "Love is death" (*odo ye wu*), and "God created death, and death killed God" (Nyame *bo owu, owu na okun*). These paradoxical statements go to show that God is the giver (love) as well as the taker (death) of life. The enigma, though, is that although God created death which in turn killed God, yet God is *Odomankoma* (eternal) and therefore not subject to death. For the Akan people death (*owu*) and God are two sides of the same phenomenon, that is, death is *odomankoma*, hence *odomankoma owu* (eternal or everlasting death).

Another evidence for the eternity of God in relation to death is expressed aphoristically as: "When God dies, I will be dead already" (*Nyame bowu no na m'ewu*). In other words, humanity's extinction is possible only via God's own demise, which is impossible. It further suggests that without God humans could not exist. Since God is eternal, in spite of the fact that God is death, it follows that humanity's continued existence is assured.

So in the final analysis God is eternal, whether as love or death. And this unique quality is what God unilaterally and graciously endows humanity with, as we will see below.

As we have seen, the Akan people contend that every person is the child of God; none is the child of the earth. That is, God is the progenitor of everything in the same way that the father is said to be the progenitor of every child. Like the father, God sustains existence with the very gift of life. This leads us to examine the divine elements in the basis of holistic personality.

We have already established the basis for the material and spiritual sources of the personality. However, there is a crucial, indispensable third entity, which, together with the material and spiritual, join to form the complete and animated human being. The relationship of the material, spiritual, and divine in the individual is sympathetic: one gives indication of the other. Birth defects are believed to be caused by asymmetry in the relationship between the three constituents of the personality.

The Okra

Life is made possible by Nana Nyame, who endows the individual with a soul, intelligence, and an existential purpose. The soul is called *okra*. The *okra* is the very essence of God in human beings and all living things and maintains its immaculate purity throughout the existence of the person or thing. The *okra* is the palpitation of all existence. Therefore it would be absurd for the Akan to say that a child is born with an "original sin." However, the bad acts (*suban bon*) of a person, learned during the maturational processes, have direct bearing on the *okra*, causing it to be grievous or sad. Individuals showing neurotic tendencies may be said to be grieving (*nekra ridze awerehow*), that is, the soul is sad. Here we see illustrated the relationship between the *wer* and the *okra* already discussed. To rejuvenate a sad, grieving soul, family members perform rites to propitiate it.

Having observed many such rites performed for relatives and non-relatives alike, I have no doubt that the rites are efficacious. Expected by loved ones to be well and happy, the individual responds. The ceremony focuses a family's attention on the subject and helps him or her to regain balance.

These rites reveal the location of the soul. Contrary to Gyekye's assertion that the soul is lodged in the head,[2] from the rite of restoration it is determined that the soul is located on the shoulders, which are appropriately called *kra-do* (place, seat, or residence of the soul). After all, the rite is intended to re-establish for the soul homeostasis with other agencies of the personality, and the shoulders signify this balance. As part of the process, the shoulders are touched with eggs when the rite is performed. Other indications of the location of the soul are the prohibitions the Akan people place on the shoulders. One must not lean upon another person's shoulders. When a shoulder is touched unwittingly, it is advisable that the other shoulder be touch for symmetry. For instance, one of the ways out of spirit possession is tapping on the shoulders of the possessed with special vines.

Another essence of the soul is that it is also known as *otseasefo* (resident one). To call the soul *otseasefo* is to affirm the eternal nature of the soul because anyone imbued with a soul is alive. For instance, when an infant dies at birth it is said that it did not come to "stay." Similarly, an infant that survives is said to have come to "reside" or live, alluding to the soul as a living entity.

In evidence of the soul as a living entity or that which resides, there is a residue in feces called *kraben*. Various discussants have described the *kraben* as whitish, grayish, yellowish, or even black excrement that remains in people or animals until death. In the act of dying, the *kraben* is often forcibly expelled. One might hear in reference to a dying person or an animal that has been hit by a vehicle: "The soul's excrement has been discharged." Such references mark the imminent departure of the soul. Conditions of death may be so painful and sudden for some that they discharge their soul feces orally. This excrement, like the soul itself that resides in the person, is not supposed to be expelled until death. Since the absence of the soul means death, it follows that its presence in the individual is tantamount to life, the very essence of the eternal, God.

Yet the Akan people also believe that the soul can be put to flight (*ne kra eguan*), its flight putting the individual under threat of imminent demise. This notion is predicated upon the understanding that the soul can be grieved, as shown above. The soul is said to be in flight when an individual is incarcerated, or when a person experiences a hierophany, such as experienced by the Apostle Paul or the Prophet Moses. Such an encounter requires the soul to be brought back or restored by offering a sacred meal to anyone believed to be in such a state. It must be stressed that failure to recognize and treat such a depressed condition leads to melancholia and may ultimately lead to death. The first step in addressing this religio-psychological condition is for the individual to recognize that the soul is in flight.

The Ahom

The evidence of the soul in the person, though intangible, is the *ahom* or *honhom* (breath). The Akan people view the continuous locomotion of inhaling and exhaling to be unquestionably God. No matter how deeply one exhales, there remains within a residual breath, attesting to the fact that the soul is eternally seated in the individual. When exhaled, the breath joins the atmosphere, that body of air which is "God without."

To the Akan people God is the air, and the air is synonymous with God. This forms the basis for the aphorism: "Speak to the wind if one wants to talk to God" (*se pede kasa kyere* Nyame *a kakyere mframa*). God then could not be aloof or a distant God when experienced both within and without as the very air that sustains life. In extension, this is the sense behind the maxim: "God is self-revealing even to a child" (*obi nnkyere abofra* Nyame). If God is self-evident and accessible to all, then the impertinence of clergy, temples, and images for God is revealed.

As breath indicates life, so the cessation of breath is death. At a time decreed only by God, the living soul (*okra tseasefo*) terminates the body when the last puff of breath is exhaled by a dying person. Nevertheless, the breath is not the soul, even though the two are intrinsically and symbiotically related. The palpitation of the heart attests to the soul (breath), and at death the soul returns to God via the breath.

If the *ahom* or breath is the intangible attestation to the soul, then the *mogya* or blood is the visible attestation to the soul. The Akan people equate blood with life, meaning that it is inherently related to the soul. Moreover, the relationship between the blood and life means that any animal for consumption must have its throat cut and some blood poured to the ground and covered. Otherwise, the meat is considered blood meat (*mogya nam*) and must not be eaten. In the past the people never ate meat thought to be blood meat because it contained the life of that animal. Nowadays, unfortunately, people eat meat sold at market places and roadside stands that may be blood meat. From the ritual perspective, to cut the throat of an animal or a person is to allow the soul to depart. The highest and purest sacrifice of any kind involves blood, the life and soul of a person or animal. Thus when the blood of a person or animal is collected for religious rites, it must remain uncoagulated by adding salt or it must be used immediately. The reference to blood here must be understood in the context of the mother. That is, it takes divine attributes to give life to the inanimate blood of the mother.

The Nkrabea

Kofi Appiah-Kubi sums up the nature of the *nkrabea* as follows:

> It is said that when God gives the *okra*, He also gives *nkrabea* ('destiny'). No one knows or can change one's destiny except God. Destiny… is concerned with the general quality and ultimate end of life. Thus, the Akans say…'when one was taking leave of one's God no one was there.' Some people are destined to be healthy, strong, hard-working, honest, and wealthy; others are destined to be sickly, weak, lazy, poor, and dishonest. One's destiny can only change when one is born again after death.[3]

Etymologically, the *nkrabea* is the conjugation of *nkra* (message) and *bea* (place, residence, journey or destination). However, it would be wrong to base the meaning solely on this conjugation. That is to say that when people talk about the concept *nkrabea*, such a conjugation is far from their thoughts. The *nkrabea* is the personalized content, meaning, and purpose of being. There is a reason and a purpose for being born; a sense of duty and mission that must be accomplished existentially. And until that is achieved one feels unfulfilled in life, but the problem is how.

The individual is endowed with ethical existence and generativity (*obra bo*), that is, a way of achieving the existential purpose of one's being. However, it does not guarantee the individual the kind of ethic to be led, except to say that there is a path to realizing the ideal existence. The tantalizing problem is that the contents of the purpose of being could only be deciphered by God. Although individualistic, the existential purpose of being must conform with societal ethos. Although shrouded in mystery, society's role is indispensable in the development of a person toward the realization of one's purpose of being.

The content of the purpose of being is simply voluminous (*nkrabea musem dooso*), yet it remains enigmatic to the individual who is obliged to fulfill them nonetheless. Failure to fulfill a purpose of being means that the individual must be reincarnated as many times as necessary in order to achieve whatever was decreed by God in the beginning. However, unlike the conception of reincarnation in some Eastern religions where the individual may be reincarnated into, say, an animal until such time as it is finally reincarnated a human being, the Akan people will always reincarnate as human beings to continue from where they left off. This freedom the individual has. So in the end there is a universal salvation for all, not for a select few as Calvinism teaches.

The *nkrabea* always accompanies the soul, thus making the soul the bearer of the distinctly personalized purpose of existence. To say that God is cognizant of one's purpose of existence means that God has foreknowledge of what sort of life the individual will have before they are born. God does not intervene or control one's ethical existence and generativity. The individual has freedom to determine and shape his or her own ethic. Yes, the Akan people are communistic socially, but when it comes to ethical existence and generativity (*obra bo*) they are very individualistic. This is because everyone is trying to find his or her niche in the world and upon finding it they return to ameliorate the community.

God endows the individual with the ability to choose their activities on earth. Often people will say to an incorrigible person: "Ethical existence is how you lead it" (*obra nye woara abo*) as a warning for a person to re-examine his or her ethics. Prior to marriage, the individual is free from ethical responsibilities, as the individual may at that time still be under tutelage of his or her parents. Upon marriage and adulthood, the individual assumes full responsibilities and must lead an ethic within the societal ethos. This individualized ethic is what determines the precise nature of an existential purpose of being, whether unethical (*bon*) or ideal (*pa*).

In the final analysis, *nkrabea* and its role in human activity may be said to be a matter of trial and error. If the individual enjoys a considerable degree of prosperity, it is attributed to his or her *nkrabea*. Likewise, if a person finds oneself in a perpetual cycle of failures, the culprit is also the *nkrabea*. The fact is that some are born to be wealthy, poor, sick, healthy, happy, sad, childless, and every human condition imaginable. This does not mean, however, that the individual is resigned to one state of existence. Only death, the eschatological component of *nkrabea*, puts an end to life's goal. And even this is decreed by the individual's purpose of being.

The inherently good thing about *nkrabea* is its universal salvivic appeal. An individual has many chances of starting over again until such time that everyone in the end attains his or her existential goal. The good news is that one should not resign oneself to any one unproductive state, but must move on and work indefatigably to improve on his or her condition. This is the very nature of *nkrabea*.

The Adwen and the Nyansa

One day an elder explained to me how knowledge is distinctly different from wisdom and intelligence (*adwen nko, nyansa nko*). But wisdom and intelligence are dependent on knowledge, the accrued body of life's experience from which intelligence and wisdom emanates.

The difference between the *adwen* (knowledge) and the *nyansa* (intelligence) is whether or not a person can make intelligent or wise decisions. A person may demonstrate a considerable amount of intelligence but may be deficient in problem-solving. The elder's statement may be made in praise of a person who exhibits both knowledge and intelligence. Often this is said in reference to those who are adept in oratory, especially during deliberation.

Both knowledge and intelligence are developmental in nature, reaching full expression in individuals who mature to eldership. Yet age alone does not qualify one for attainment of this station. The person who does not exhibit mental maturity and acuity is excluded from the company of elders. The older person who lacks common sense is referred to as useless (*opanyin gyangen*) or foolish or stupid (*kwasiampanyin*).

To say that knowledge and intelligence are developmental suggests that they are innately present from birth onwards. Thus parents often ask their insolent child: "Where is your sense?" or "Are you out of your mind?" These interrogations go to show that even from an early age the child's moral conduct must be governed by both knowledge and intelligence. Any aberration from the expected norms of behavior is seen as an inherent absence of knowledge and intelligence. Conversely, a youth who demonstrates all the right social etiquettes characterized by respect for the elders is said to be intelligent and a thinker (*obadwenmafo*). Such a youth is always accorded the honor of sitting with the elders, as expressed in the following: "The hygienic youth dines with the elders." However, a foolish person is shunned by his or her peers, as revealed in the maxim: "The undisciplined elder is reviled by children."

The two parental admonitions of wayward children quoted above allude to the location of knowledge and intelligence. In fact, both are thought to be inside the head, controlling every human activity and thought. While it is impossible to determine the precise niche of intelligence, knowledge is said to be the brain, notwithstanding. For example, the mudfish is called *adwen* and from time immemorial it has been used in Akan political thought to symbolize intelligence and judiciousness because of its big head. The Akan people believe that the bigger the head, the larger the brain size and therefore the more intelligent and knowledgeable one is. This has given rise to the saying: "Big head has brains" (*tsir kesi na adwen wom*).

Most children, including myself, eat the brains of fish, hoping to augment their own brain size. Children have small knowledge at birth, but are expected to gain with physical growth the mental acuity consistent with the increase of knowledge.

A fine distinction is drawn between knowledge and intelligence, but in the end they constitute an inseparable entity. Distinctions are made when one fails to show the cognitive capabilities of expected levels of maturity. Intelligence, then, is the ethereal aspect of knowledge, manifesting itself in adulthood and old age as wisdom.

N o t e s

1. See Henry Meredith, *An Account of the Gold Coast of Africa: With a Brief History of the African Company* (London: Frank Cass & Co. Ltd., [1812] (1967). For further discussions see Ellis, op.cit.; Rattray, op.cit.; Busia, op.cit.; Gyekye, op.cit. (to name but a few).
2. Gyekye, op. cit., p. 100.
3. Appiah-Kubi, *Man Cures, God Heals*, pp. 10-11.

PART II
CHILDHOOD

C h a p t e r   6

C H I L D H O O D
S P I R I T U A L I T Y

Childbirth is exclusively a female social event and men are not allowed into the delivery house. Some men may linger around in case they are needed. Often, when complications arise during parturition, the father is called in to pour libations to mitigate the spirit of the unborn child and facilitate parturition. Psychologically, the father's presence facilitates parturition when the woman knows that her husband is nearby.

Upon hearing that his wife has delivered safely, the husband sends an old but clean cloth of his to his wife to be used as a pillow for the neonate. The cloth is imbued with the father's fully developed spirit to serve as a buttress against evil spirits capable of causing harm to the neonate's weaker spirit. This ritual instills faith, hope, and security for the family in knowing that the neonate is protected spiritually by, at times, an absent father.

Following this, a welcoming (*ahohow ye*) rite may be performed by the father. The father welcomes the new arrival by purchasing pairs of items needed by the neonate, including kerosene, soaps, sponges, towels, etc. These items, together with chickens, are sent to his wife. In contemporary practice this rite may be deferred until the naming rite on the eighth day, but fathers who ignore this rite may be reviled by their peers for failing to live up to their responsibility.

The Akan attach great importance to the first baths of the neonate. The crucial nature of these baths is such that the grandmother or an experienced woman offers them. For instance, an individual who emits bad odor during perspiration is thought not to have received a clean, thorough first bath. Before the naval cord drops off, extra care is taken to ensure that the wound is not affected by water. Afterwards, the neonate is bathed at least twice a day with emphasis on the morning baths. These baths become the norm throughout life, with the adult expected to take two baths—morning and evening—every day.

The Akan people are obsessed with the physical structure of a person. Thus, beginning with the neonate, they do their best to remold it into a socially accepted physical form. The ritual of remolding commences with the first baths and is intended to ensure physiological alignments. Beginning with the head the neonate is placed face-up on the lap of an adept, its head towards the knees. Dipping a towel into a lukewarm water and squeezing, the grandmother caresses the neonate, starting with the head. The aim is to remold the head into an accepted shape: round for the Akan people to the south and oval for those to the north. The massage continues meticulously for as long as necessary, while making sure that water does not get into the ears. When satisfied with her work, the grandmother oils and combs the infant's hair.

Additional hot water may be added to the existing water to stroke the neonate's hands several times from the shoulder to the fingers. This ritual is repeated on the stomach, ribs, back, and legs until every part of the body has been stroked thoroughly. Afterwards the infant may be held by the hand or leg and suspended upside down momentarily in the air. Or the infant may be thrown up about two or three times in the air aimed at introducing it to heights. Another reason is for the infant to overcome fear.

Finally, the neonate is bathed, dressed, fed, and put to sleep on its back or side. The entire ritual of remolding and bathing may take about an hour or so every morning. I have observed in some cases that the remainder of the water in the bucket is used to wash other siblings of the neonate. One reason may be spiritual as well as physical bonding of siblings, but a more pragmatic reason, I believed, is water conservation.

Throughout these daily rituals the biological mother watches curiously and attentively for the first few weeks. Gradually she assumes control, but still under the probing eyes of older women for any potentially harmful handling of the neonate by the mother. This ritual may continue for three months.

These pedagogical rituals inculcate the processes of mothering. It is simply not enough to say that motherhood is the experience of gestation, parturition, and lactation. It encompasses observation of neonatal care given to the mother's own infant by experienced mothers during the crucial first trimester, post-partum care, and the care the young mother herself gave to her younger siblings when she was a teenager by carrying infants on her back.

Infant girls have their ears pierced during the first few weeks after delivery. In most cases the piercing is performed by placing the bark of a freshly peeled plantain on the back of the ears and piercing with a needle at the lower tip of the ears. As the needle is pulled back the holes are believed to be disinfected by the chemical content of the plantain bark. Moreover, the bark cushions the ears as they are small and protects the officiant's fingers from being pierced. Then a black thread is passed through the holes and tied to prevent blockage while the wounds are healed. The wounds may be dressed several times a day with a black palm kernel oil due to its incredible healing effect. After the wounds are completely healed, ear rings are put in.

Threaded white beads are put on the neonate's wrists, neck, waist, knees, and ankles and changed accordingly with growth. Since cloth diapers are used the beads around the waist can serve as suspenders for the diapers. Girls and women must wear beads around their waist throughout adulthood as a mark of their femininity. This is the reason behind the proverbial saying: "The beads of the ideally sensuous woman are silent" (*Ahondze pa nnkasa*) when her spouse caresses them during their romantic rendezvous. All kings, the clergy, and elders must wear specially made beads around their wrists always. Boys may be circumcised at the discretion of their parents because there is no organized rite involving circumcision.

The spirituality of infants is evidenced by the notion that the neonates are thought to be spiritual personalities originating from the ancestral world. This goes to confirm the tangibility of the spiritual personality. The duration of the neonate's spiritual personality status in the temporal lasts until the beginning of awareness. Then it begins to be conscious of itself as an object having a body in relation to others. That is, it sees itself in totality apart from others, but in relationship to the matrikin.

The process of severance with the ancestral world and the ushering into the mundane is a slow process, however. Depending on the maturational progress of an infant, it could take up to six years. In the meanwhile, the infant keeps close contact with its spiritual siblings with whom it plays, especially when people perceive it to be alone. In this way, the infant is never alone because it is surrounded by numerous invisible playmates with whom it communicates telepathically.

My discussants believe that infants are happiest when they are alone. They point out that sometimes when infants are alone they may be discovered laughing or smiling, making gestures that indicate engagement with someone, and crying for no apparent provocation. These attest to the fact that they are in the company of their spiritual siblings and spiritual mother.

Infants, the elders maintain, are acutely aware of their surroundings in both the temporal and the spiritual worlds. Ironically, they are born blind to the mundane world. Awareness is not always commensurate with sight, and this is exactly the state in which the infant is believed to be. Infants are born blind because their visual perceptions, although inherently present, are slight in comparison with those of adults. The way to determine their non-perceptibility is by moving a finger or hand across their face or eyes to precipitate blinking. Some infants are born with their eyes opened but that does not mean that they can see. This initial blindness is believed to last for about six weeks. The duration of the blindness, my discussants insist, has decreased significantly from about three months to six weeks or less. To compensate for the absence of perception, infants respond to stimuli acoustically so that they can discern voices in infancy. By coordinating certain touching with specific sounds infants can respond warmly to the embrace of friendly touches.

The decreased period of blindness is attributed to reincarnation for two reasons. First, the same children are being reincarnated; and second, that there is famine in the ancestral world and therefore the need to reincarnate. What these suggest is that because the same children are being reincarnated into a world they already know, there is no reason to prolong blindness. If they are born primarily for food, then they need not be blind for too long since they have to start searching for food soon after birth. What is implied here is that children these days mature more quickly and faster in order to compete for a limited amount of resources in the world.

Prior to perception the infant is considered to be in a state of darkness. Gradually everything appears in black and white or contrasts. Sooner or later dark shades become distinguishable to the extent that faces can be discerned and appreciated, e.g., a smile from a familiar face. Prior to this point, however, infants do not coordinate and reciprocate the mother's facial expression. When they smile, they do so instinctively and indiscriminately.

Further evidence of the dark and light phenomenon is explained by the irrelevance of time for neonates. During the period of blindness neonates cannot distinguish between night and day. They may sleep and wake up at any time of the day or night. My discussants contend they regulate infants' sleeping habits by curtailing sleeping time during the day. By the end of the first trimester infants seem to find their place in the natural order of things, discerning day-light from night-darkness.

With the gradual increase of light, night-darkness recedes to a point where light is associated with locomotion and darkness with rest. By the beginning of the second trimester, infants can distinguish colors and personalities. From three months onwards, mothers, adults, and sisters begin to carry infants on their back so that infants can discern smells and show their predilection for select objects or personalities. Infants might not sleep well when put suddenly on a different mat that may not emit the same urine smell, for instance. Or, when introduced to angry, bearded faces they are not accustomed to seeing they may turn away in flight and cry. It is not unusual to notice a child crying when being taken away by an unfamiliar individual and stretching out its hands towards its mother or a familiar person for help.

As they probe the faces of their primary caretakers they scan with precision facial features, voice pitch, and tonality. All objects and personalities are fixated at this point, because when in flight they always turn to the directions they believe the fixated objects are found for safety. This is possible because they internalize all significant points of reference and cry or crawl toward them when agitated.

Child-care is a communal effort and everyone lends a hand in the process. At the end of the first three months the mother is strong enough to attend to her daily tasks, including carrying the baby around on her back.

To carry an infant on the back a helper may be needed initially due to the tender nature of infants. The mother bends over just enough for the baby to remain stationary on her back. The baby's legs are spread apart in such a way that they point straight and rest on either side of the mother's waist. Then a first piece of cloth (*ahatado*) is placed over the infant and knotted at the mother's chest and waist, respectively. This first piece of cloth is the main support for the infant. With the exception of the head every part is tied firmly inside the cloth. Afterwards a second piece of cloth is tied over the first to give it added security. Because the neck is tender, care is taken during the tying so that the neck is firmly secured.

As the infant grows older the mother does not need assistance in carrying the child on her back. After the second trimester, most mothers are able to place the child on their backs unassisted. The mother passes the child under her left arm and grips the child's hands under her armpits. Simultaneously she pulls the pieces of cloth loosely tied to her waist over the child and knots them. The older child's hand may be left untied until it falls asleep. They are then put inside the cloth and tied together with its head.

The affection that exists between the mother and the child on her back cannot be overemphasized. The child is bonded physically to its mother in such a way that it feels the warmth, assurance, security, and a sense of belonging. It can always bury its head on its mother's back inside the cloth or turn its head away from envious children who may try to establish eye contact. From the child's vantage point it is a feeling of superiority in relation to other children below.

At about age four I was still carried by my paternal grandmother, to the envy of many youngsters. A few adults pulled my legs, teasing her that I was too old to be carried around. Of course my grandmother did not think so and angrily protested. But while on her back I felt so pompously possessive of her that I would not want to get down when she got tired.

From the mother's perspective, carrying the child is for convenience and mobility, especially when travelling, working, or engaged in her household chores. When the child becomes listless, grouchy, or peevish the mother will pick the child up and carry it on her back where the child may sleep. There is a sense of possession; the child belongs to her exclusively until such time as it becomes physically impossible to carry it any longer. As if to compensate for the strain of carrying babies, there appears to be some gratification as the mother is affected by every tickling sensation or movement while the baby is on her back.

Lactation may take as long as necessary. Mothers breast-feed their babies anywhere and whenever needed. Even when children are on the backs of their mothers, the breast is readily available when needed. Any inclination towards hunger prompts the mother to untie the cloths holding the child on her back, pass the child under her arm to her side and commence to suckle it. It is not uncommon to see a mother carrying a heavy load and concurrently suckling her baby. Most adults do not particularly perceive bare breasts as objects of shame.

Lactation may also serve as a pacifier for an especially irritable infant. Sometimes because the breasts are readily available infants become possessive of them and oblivious to the fact that they belong to the mother. But such a child soon realizes that the breasts are not objects to be possessed, for its sadistic behavior may lead to early weaning as the mother may smear bitter substances on her nipples.

During the weaning process the child may not only lose the breasts but also reject the mother for having broken trust. The child may reach out for alternative mothers, i.e., grandmothers, readily available in any given household. I have observed alternative mothers suckling children who are undergoing weaning even though no milk was available in their breasts. The aim is simply to pacify the child's insatiable craving for the breasts during this difficult period. With time, children return to their mothers, reconciled to the loss of the breast. Trust is restored.

Toilet training begins early. Cloth diapers are used by handing them around the waist beads from behind the infant and passing them through its legs. These cloth diapers are very porous. Thus it is not uncommon to notice mothers wet at the waist level.

As soon as an infant's neck is strong enough to support its head, the infant is introduced to the chamber-pot and held while sitting on it to prevent it from falling over. This may be done several times a day until such time as that child is able to associate bowel movement with the pot unassisted. However, in the absence of a chamber-pot the mother tilts the soles of her feet up for the infant to sit on while holding it. From early on the child learns to associate this sitting posture with the need to toilet. Having been taught this way, children later on use chamber-pots unassisted or simply get behind a house at a designated place and squat to toilet.

Children treat their excrement with disdain at an early age because they are prevented from coming into contact with their excrement. If a child unwittingly gets in contact with its feces, then (it is believed) its soul has "departed" and must be "brought back" by the giving of a boiled egg to the child to eat. Furthermore, if some of an infant's feces inadvertently gets into food, the food is not thrown away but is eaten after the portion contaminated is cleaned and thrown away. To throw away all of the food is tantamount to rejecting the infant.

With regard to urination, children who continue to wet themselves at night will be awakened and asked to use the chamber-pot. Continued urination may result in public humiliation, such as happened to me when I was about five years old. One morning after wetting myself, an aunt of mine came and wrapped my mat around me and placed me in the middle of the compound as my peers hooted at me. After a while my paternal grandmother came to my rescue; I cannot recall if I ever wet myself again. The shame I felt was simply overwhelming.

By the end of the sixth month children have already learned how to sit up. It begins with the child being taught how to sit up on the ground or floor and attended by an older child who sits behind the infant as a buttress. Infants lean forward and when they sit up straight may fall backwards for lack of balance. Initially infants are not allowed to sit up for extended periods for fear of straining their backs. In the absence of caretakers, the mother usually places the child in a tray buttressed with pillows. This practice frees the mother to carry on her chores while still watching her child.

As infants master the art of sitting up, they become more and more focused and industrious. When bright or colored objects are put before them their inclination is to reach those targets. Although focused, their reflexivity is not coordinated. They may reach their intended objects alright but cannot hold on to them firmly; whenever it appears that they have a firm grip, the objects simply fumble in their hands. Although unable to hold on firmly to their objects and coordinate their action, they are persistent and may not forego their goal until disinterested or when those objects disappear. But the area is fixated so that whenever another opportunity arises they may want to explore the same area again. The objects when reached almost invariably find their way into the child's mouth. The object-to-mouth coordination facilitates the child's ability to feed itself by the end of the fourth trimester when food is placed before it. The pursuit of objects also prepares children for the locomotive phase of the developmental process, crawling.

Children are allowed to crawl freely on open compounds but always within the range and eyesight of adults. As they begin to pursue their targets and sit up to examine them, one cannot but notice how they soil themselves. Although they have latitude to move around on the open ground, they do so cautiously, all the time looking back to ascertain the omnipresence of trusted ones, regardless of how far they might have gone. Consequently, should they encounter any frightful experience, they always return to the safety of trusted ones. Conversely, when they encounter any frightening experiences out of sight and range of trusted ones, they panic. Fear sets in, and they cry for help. The very nature of surfaces make children susceptible to injuries. Sometimes children are pierced by a bone or sharp objects such as a broken glass, pin or sharp stones in the palm, knee, feet, or even the stomach.

At the beginning of the "fourth trimester" most children are attempting to walk or are able to stand up by holding on to stationary objects. One way of assisting a child to walk is for an adult to hold both hands of the child while the adult moves backwards.

As soon as a child takes its first steps unilaterally, a boiled egg may be given to it as reward for its soul. From now on adults encourage the child to take more steps by extending their hands to the child to hold yet pulling back simultaneously. In this way more steps are taken by the child until such time as the child masters the act of walking.

Chapter 7

EDUCATION

> O God my God, what miseries and mockeries did I now experience, when obedience to my teachers was proposed to me, as proper in a boy, in order that in this world I might prosper, and excel in tongue-science, which should serve to the praise of men, and to deceitful riches. Next I was put to school to get learning, in which I (poor wretch) knew not what use there was; and yet, if idle in learning, I was beaten. For this was judged right by our forefathers; and many, passing the same course before us, framed for us weary paths, through which we were fain to pass.[1]

St. Augustine's succinct description of his harsh boyhood training is remarkably akin to the Akan educational stage despite the vast geographical difference and history between West and North Africa. I telephoned a relative of mine in Ghana and asked about his daughter. He told me that she was no longer staying with him. Then his wife interjected to say: "She must be trained." My relative and his wife, who are wealthy, believed that they had indulged their only daughter. So they sent her away to live with a friend of theirs whom they believed would not pamper her.

Why do couples and even families send their children away to stay with others, voluntarily or involuntarily? The key word here is *ntsetsee*, that is, to train or rear. By *ntsetsee* I mean learning all about ethical existence and generativity, and the pedagogy of cognitive development. Hence this stage indicates the school or educational period, as tests will show below. The educational period is a difficult stage, sharply in contrast with the pampered, loving childhood. For one thing, it is characterized by austerity because the child's moral character begins to be formed. That is probably why this stage is communal in nature. This point was brought home to me one day when an old woman said to me: "No single person rears a child." But until this woman told me this I had not cogitated upon the way children were raised as teenagers. The older woman proceeded to complain to me about her difficulty in getting her granddaughter of twelve to obey her or to do anything. She felt that the girl had reached a crucial point in her development and without the influence of someone authoritative enough to impose proper discipline, her future marriage would prove difficult.

In retrospect I empathize with her. She reminds me of my paternal grandmother who had painfully parted with me because others felt she pampered me. She had every reason to hang on to me; after all my father, her last born, had died and under no circumstance would she lose me. One day my uncle, who lived about two miles away, came and seized me by the hands and spanked me severely. Not long after that he came for me. It is hard to say what would have happened if my uncle had not come to fetch me. I would have otherwise been left to my own devices. One change that came of the experience was that I became a disciplined boy.

Obedience and respect for the elders and authority, the ideal ethical existence and generativity, and the acquisition of wisdom and intelligence at adulthood are the goals of the educational period. When people like the older woman and my grandmother feel they have lost control of their wards, they capitulate to relatives in the hope of rearing the children into obedient and respectful future citizens. To capitulate to this separation does not mean failure; it is, rather, recognizing one's limitations and knowing when to ask for communal participation in the educational processes. In the case of incorrigible children, they are sent to live with distant relatives to serve (*som*) until they cultivate the proper moral character attributes.

The improper display of social mores by children is perceived as a direct indictment of their parents, obvious in questions like: "Were you not trained properly?" "Who trained you?" "Are you out of your mind?" and "Where are your senses?" These statements go to show that the moral and ethical conduct of children is intertwined with their cognitive development. That is, they must exhibit the cognition commensurate with maturation because knowledge and intelligence are developmental in nature, as we have seen above. On the other hand, well disciplined children may be thought of as well trained and are often commended for their manners. Such children are said to have demonstrated the proper cognition and are perceived as thinkers already. When they inadvertently violate the rules of conduct, their relatives often come to their defense.

Punishment must follow the child's insolence immediately, for any abeyance fails to register the cause-and-effect relationship. It is only later that an explanation might be necessary. Nevertheless, spanking or whipping is not carried out indiscriminately on any part of the child's body, otherwise the parents may encounter the wrath of other family members. The custom is that children are spanked on the buttocks or on the palm with a cane.

One aspect of the educational period in relation to punishment is that the child is punished when wrong but not necessarily rewarded when right. In practice, this often means that the child will be corrected through punishment when social rules are contravened but not necessarily taught what those rules of conduct are. The right and proper way is for the child to observe, imitate, and accompany adults obediently until such time as the child has acquired all skills necessary to embark on an ethic geared to the good of the matrikin folks.

Along the same lines restitutions are not made when a child unwittingly causes physical damage to another. Any recompense is deemed insulting to the victim since certain losses are irreplaceable. Childhood naiveté is a shared phenomenon, meaning, any child can cause unintended injury to another person or property. A child therefore cannot be liable for mishaps since it is understood that any child is capable of such acts. Such a child is not exculpated, however. The parents who feel responsible will surely reprimand the child for not applying common sense but will not pay damages unless the victim demands it, which sometimes happens.

A child is always in a position of shame before adults. The child lowers his or her head and avoids looking up straight into the adult's face. There are times when the child may look at the face of the adult, that is, when the child is receiving instructions or being sent, but even here the child avoids direct eye contact with the adult. In fact, the child who habitually gazes on the faces of adults is deemed a witch. And in any case, children must look down and must not talk back to adults. The rule of thumb is that a child never speaks to an elder until the child is first spoken to by an elder.

Children are not allowed in the company of adults, and when adults gather for discussion children may not pass between them but rather behind, if possible. Otherwise the child must wait until granted permission to pass. The child is likewise not to interrupt or interject when adults are engaged in conversation. The prudent child may use gestures to draw the attention of an adult, quite often unbeknownst to those present. Or, the child may approach another elder and ask him or her to call or convey a message to the intended adult. However, when these two steps fail, then the child will have to wait until such time as the adults are finished with their discussion.

Children must never refer to adults by name directly. Adults inculcated this practice by referring to other adults by the names of their children or other relatives. If the child is asked by another adult as to where he or she had been, the child's response would be: " My mother sent me to Kweku's father's house." To refer to an adult by name, a qualifier is used. An adult may say to a child: "Take this money to Maame Atta." Or the child will say: "Papa Kwame says I should bring these fruits to you." This does not mean that children do not know the names of their parents or adults, but for a child to refer to an adult by name is considered an affront to the intended adult. In the eyes of an adult a son or daughter is always a child, even in adulthood.

To speak to or ask favors from adults, the child must use two specific forms of address: "please" (*mepa wo kyow*) and "thank you" (*meda wo ase*). The pleases and thank-yous are expressions of humility and graciousness by a well-disciplined person toward significant others.

Another way of expressing appreciation for one's generosity towards another may not be spontaneous but deferred overnight.

Although the initial expression of appreciation will be expressed immediately, the final expression of gratitude will be delayed until the morrow.

Gifts should be received with both hands or the right hand only. The use of the left hand in many functions, including eating and the reception of gifts, is a taboo. If a left-handed person stretches his or her left hand unintentionally to another when offering assistance, the other person will not reach out in return. At an early age children born with left-hand proclivities are encouraged to use the right hand instead. What then is inherently wrong with the left hand? The left hand implies disrespect, shame, desecration, and arrogance, and should not be used in such a way as to communicate insolence. The left hand is regarded as ritually impure because it is used for anal cleansing, among other things. To use it to show or point at people or objects signifies profound disrespect and condescension towards the intended person or object.

When our twins were born and were still in the hospital, my wife and I decided not to allow the pastor of the church we attended to baptize them because he was left-handed. Our decision was engendered by our desire to adhere to our tradition. For us, such a numinous rite requires the highest religious efficacy of the parties involved. If the pastor's use of the left hand would cause the rite to lose its religious efficacy, then the decision not to baptize the children was the right one.

However, there are exceptional moments when the left hand is used without evoking its condescending connotations. When a person cannot use the right hand for one reason or another, then the left hand's auxiliary role is accepted without reservation. The person who cannot receive something with the right hand, for instance, will receive with the left hand but not before the right hand has been placed underneath the left with an apology: "Excuse my left hand." Similarly, when gifts are to be dispensed the same ritual is followed. To the recipient no offense is meant and none is taken since this ritual is equivalent to the use of the right hand. Even when the right hand is not used for support, the apologetic words suffice. This is the only way the left hand may be used to receive or dispense gifts, items, or money.

Another cosmetic rite has to do with dental hygiene. Children are not expected to speak to anyone when they wake up in the morning. The first mandatory ritual is to wash one's face, mouth, and chew a stick or sponge to clean the teeth. Often bitter, these chewing sticks and sponges are believed to prevent cavities and whiten teeth. Some people may chew their stick or sponge for several hours and take them out when they have to eat or drink. The fact is that children who dare break this early morning ritual run the risk of being punished by being denied food.

Greetings are mandatory. Failure to greet or respond when greeted is a sign of disrespect, hostility, and anger towards the other. Sometimes a person may demand to know why such treatment is warranted. Verbal greetings may be followed by hand shakes by gripping and twisting each other's middle finger to create a popping sound upon snapping the fingers. This denotes comradery and public display of affection toward each other. Hugging, albeit uncommon, is carried out among close relatives. Persons of the same sex can hold hands to display their love and affection for each other without the slightest overtones of homosexuality.

Most children grow up in female households or are taught most of what they will later use in their adult lives by women. The long lactation period allows women to exercise considerable power over children early in life and during the educational period. For instance, the division of labor for boys and girls is laid down early, commencing with the ability to comprehend and carry out instruction. This is marked by the child's capability to run errands without any serious omissions.

Fathers begin to play a greater role in the lives of their boys at a later stage. As soon as boys are able to understand formal instructions, they are allowed to carry meals to their fathers, who may live apart from their wives. Once there, the boys may eat the meal with their fathers and later return the dishes to their mothers. Even where parents live in the same household, boys tend to eat with their fathers while girls eat with their mothers.

The father now begins his son's formal training to acquire certain knowledge in, say, fishing, farming, carpentry, etc. To learn a father's profession is to accompany him wherever he goes. This enables a boy to observe his father at work and to receive theoretical instructions pertinent to the profession. At the right age the son is allowed practical application of what has been taught. A fisherman's son, for instance, receives basic fishing techniques.[2]

Girls may have limited contact with their fathers at this stage. But they enjoy the same degree of involvement with their mothers as boys do with their fathers. This is the beginning of the division of labor. Children do not have the luxury of toys. Girls in particular compensate for this by collecting empty cans as toys and playfully imitating their mothers as they cook. Their experience comes from observing their mothers prepare food and perform all the other chores associated with cooking. It is imperative that girls know how to cook and run the household. Mothers make sure girls are present when they are preparing food and doing other household chores.

Besides cooking, girls have remarkable managerial, mathematical, and economic skills. The spirit of entrepreneurship is inculcated early when children around the ages of five or six accompanying older girls, sell anything from food products to nonperishable merchandise. These goods are usually furnished by their mothers from the many market centers after selling their own products. An eight-year-old girl may sell foodstuffs, dishes, clothing, and many other items usually under the auspices of an older girl or mother. Such sales require that a substantial amount of money change hands. The girl must handle it efficiently and learn to account for every penny.

When children are given money and sent to purchase items at the market, they are required to return with all items, including the exact change. Better yet, girls must be able to memorize and ultimately internalize the recipe for the preparation of various soups and meals. Specifically, they will have to be precise with their hands in measuring such ingredients as salt, pepper, etc., in order not to make soups salty or too spicy for consumption. Girls from the age of seven and up can list most ingredients for the preparation of soups, like palm, groundnut (peanut), etc. They prepare themselves as wives by preparing food for their imaginary husbands, visitors, other children, and grandparents.

It would be counterproductive to write a list of items to be purchased when the aim is to develop the child's mental acuity by internalizing, recalling, and associating the items with certain operations. In the past, my wife has prepared several West African dishes for special occasions, and we have invited our African and non-African friends over. Some of our non-African friends would ask her for recipes for some of the meals. At first she was startled at their requests because she never used written recipes. Even after she told them how to prepare the dishes, they might still want to know how many teaspoons of salt, for instance, they should add.

After observing the interplay between mothers and children from the ages of six to fourteen as they attempted to carry out the above responsibilities, my assistants and I decided to test them out. First, we observed girls learning how to prepare foods and then asked them to list the ingredients prior to preparation of the foods, and after preparation asked them to list the items in reverse order. The process of reversibility is crucial in oral societies like the Akan, because the ability to retain countless number of proverbs as an elder and recall them spontaneously during deliberations has its genesis at the educational stage. From the cognitive operational standpoint the inability of children ten years old and under to think in reverse order means that they cannot think through any given operation. That is, they handle variables only as tangible things to be used rather than as true variables to be examined carefully before being used.

Next, we sent children to market places and asked them to purchase items needed for the preparation of different meals. Our aim was to find out how much they retained by checking the items they actually brought back against what was forgotten and, of course, the leftover change. We kept the list of items to be purchased and offered them less, equal, or more money for the items to be purchased.

Thirdly, we called in children who sold food products and non-perishable merchandise to test their mathematical skills. We bought combinations of different items at varying prices and gave them money in large bills to see how they went about computing the task and determining the right change due us. Sometimes we deliberately offered them less money in the hope of discovering if they would be able to determine the discrepancy. Other times, we gave them more money than needed for the items purchased and pretended as though the sum was correct. Again, this was to find out whether or not they would discover the discrepancy and refund the difference. One of our main concerns here was moral as well as ethical, how children made moral choices based on the problems before them and what influenced their decisions.

A twelve-year-old boy after returning from school was sent to the market by his uncle's wife. He was hungry at the time but dared not ask for food. When he came back about an hour later, he was whipped.

Upon enquiring, I was told he cheated. How did he do it? I talked to him days later, and he told me that he was hungry and figured by cheating he could buy food to eat and still purchase all the food stuffs. For instance, when told to buy ten cents worth of pepper he bought eight cents worth and so on. By buying less on items like pepper and tomatoes, which are not measured but heaped or grouped and therefore appeared plentiful, he reasoned that it would be hard to detect. He was wrong.

Another girl of fourteen went without food for a whole day for what her mother considered irresponsible behavior. She was told by her mother to go and collect a debt owed her by another woman. When she got to the other woman's house she realized that there were many people there. Not going inside the debtor's house, she returned and told her mother that the woman was not at home. Her angry mother went to the debtor's house and found her there. Thinking that her daughter had told the truth, she quarrelled with the woman. It was during their acrimonious exchange that the mother realized that her daughter had lied.

When we talked with her she admitted her guilt. She said that when she got there she felt shy upon seeing many people and had to make a decision as to whether to collect the money or to return home. Choosing the latter she had to think of a reason, hence the lie. If she had chosen the former she would have experienced the embarrassment of a debt collector, something with which she did not want to be faced, probably due to her sense of shame at her age. However, in choosing to lie she second-guessed her mother's reaction—incorrectly.

The lessons of these two cases are that children at this level are capable of making moral decisions that are pertinent to their contextual experience, no matter how sophomoric those decisions might be. The fourteen-year-old girl and the twelve-year-old boy clearly thought through their respective operations, that is, they were able to think in reverse. Spurred by the need to satisfy an urge (hunger) the boy made a decision to cheat; while the fourteen-year-old girl, faced with the potential for shame, chose to lie.

Most of the testing was done at random because we did not want to arouse suspicion or influence the outcome. Also, the paradigms used here are already in existence among the Akan people so that we simply operated within the culturally accepted paradigms to identify certain variables. Because the testing dealt with practical situations designed to lay the foundation for cognitive development and orality, we could observe children operationally as they tried to arrive at meaningful resolutions and offer us verbal responses within the fundamental medium of orality.

Samples of tests given are as follows. A seven-year-old girl was preparing palm-nut soup with leftover ingredients from her mother. She was under a tree in front of her house. She had at least four empty cans and a fire place of three stones of equal size which had small sticks of wood ready to be lit.

Author:	What are you doing?
Aba:	I am playing.
Author:	What kind of play?
Aba:	I am preparing palm-nut soup.
Author:	Can you tell me how to prepare it?
Aba:	Well! You need palm-nut, pepper, onion, tomatoes, salt, and your fish.
Author:	But I don't see any fish. [She opened another can and showed me partial smoked heads of herring]
Aba:	Then you put your pot on the fire and prepare it.
Author:	Good. Well, cook it and when I return I will come and eat some. [She smiles.]

When I returned the soup was not ready, but it was on the fire and boiling. And although she tried to recount what items were put into the boiling water in reverse order she aborted the process several times. After many tries, however, she was successful. The difficulty in recounting in reverse order was prevalent among children between the ages of six and ten, although they had less difficulty adding or listing the items. However, when asked to say how fufu is prepared and then say it in reverse order, they had no difficulty because fufu required only two ingredients. The difference is obvious: soup preparation involves several ingredients and hence the difficulty in thinking through the operation. However, the older the children (ages 10 to 14), the less difficulty there was in soup preparation and recalling of the process.

The finding was confirmed when we sent children to the markets to purchase from two to six items. The fewer the quantity, the less children between the ages of six and ten forgot. But when we increased the items to include six or more ingredients, the same children forgot at least two items. Interestingly, when they forgot they came back saying the items were out of stock; and yet when we sent them again to purchase only those items allegedly out of stock, they came back with them. Some of the children on their way to the market admitted repeating to themselves what they were to purchase, yet could not in the end recall all of the list. When pressed, they admitted that they were distracted or stopped on the way for various reasons.

Here is an example of things purchased by a nine-year-old boy:

Author: Can I send you to the market to buy me some items?
Kofi: Yes.
Author: Buy me a loaf of bread, two bags of tea, two bags of granulated sugar, three eggs, a tin of milk, two balls of kenkey, fried fish, stewed pepper with the fish, and a cup of Cocoo.

What are listed here are indicative of a typical breakfast, so that the child would not have difficulty recalling them. Our goal was not to confuse children with complicated grocery lists but rather offer them lists that they are conversant with at a given setting, such as provisions for breakfast or for evening meal. When they returned with the provisions, they had some difficulty recalling the items. It seems that after they purchased the items they repressed the thoughts and could not recall in successive order.

One reason for this may be that since most children obey and carry out the orders of adults under implied threat of punishment, there seemed to be memory blockage when suddenly obliged to recall. We think that if these children did not have to operate under threat of punishment, most would recall the items, as tests showed. In general, children under the age of ten forgot at least two items when the items were more than six, but children above the age of ten and below fifteen forgot at least one ingredient if the provisions were about a dozen. The high rate of retention by older children tested had to do with the fact that they can think in reverse. Furthermore, we operated under the assumption of reward and tipped them after every operation.

In a last test, we wanted to know if Western education, with its emphasis on writing, superseded or in any way influenced the world view, social perspective, cognitivity, and orality of children. The children tested in this study attended school in the town of Winneba. First, we gave them the option of writing short letters or delivering the same message by word of mouth. All the students opted for the latter. Their reason was that if they could say it then there was no point in writing down the message. The point is, even the educated individual when given the choice between speaking and writing will almost invariably choose the former. The reason for this phenomenon is obvious: orality.

Secondly, we tested the artistic skills of children in grades five and six or children between the ages of twelve and fourteen. We asked them to draw or paint anything of interest to them.[3] There were striking differences between the drawings produced by boys and girls. The most conspicuous difference is the contrasts of scenery. Girls portrayed domestic scenes, while boys were preoccupied with non-domestic activities. Girls' drawings depicted the family, household duties, and their conception of the ideal woman as the embellisher, sustainer, and preserver of the home.

Boys, however, depicted scenery that was mostly influenced by foreign innovations, such as airplanes, cars, ships, etc. These artistic expressions subliminally reinforced the boys' role outside the home, providing the vehicle for industrialism. In other words, boys after school are provided with all available means to pursue whatever goals they wish to outside the home, while girls are discouraged from furthering whatever career goals they may have outside the home. Clearly, the division of labor or occupational choices are deeply embedded at an early age. Even the ideal, educated woman must run the home while the man is absent. The man is perceived at the "go getter." The difference in the items shows that society reinforces the traditional roles of requiring girls to perform household duties, while allowing boys to play with their peers uninterrupted most times. In general, boys were influenced by foreign innovations. But the objects they depicted have been around for a long time and have been assimilated into the Akan ethos.

Finally, the drawings depicted religious symbols, such as church buildings. They confirm our interviews on religious ideas and symbols and show that children form ideas about religion and death very early even though they are sometimes unable to communicate them coherently. A ten-year-old girl who stole fruits from an older man's garden was told that the old man was coming to arrest her. The old man had died about two weeks earlier. She was eating a mango fruit when I saw her.

Author: The old man is coming to catch you.
Esi: No.
Author: I mean, he is coming.
Esi: He is dead!
Author: How do you know?
Esi: He slept and did not wake up.
Author: So where is he?
Esi: They took him to the cemetery.
Author: Can I find him at the cemetery?
Esi: No, he is gone to Nyankopon [God].
Author: Where is Nyankopon?
Esi: The sky.

By the end of the educational period, children may have a basic conception of death as a permanent and timeless state of sleep, but it still remains an unexplained, puzzling phenomenon. They have encountered death, for example, at funerals where they might accompany adults or go to sell their products. Perhaps with the exception of state festivals, local funerals are the most important social events for children to sell things, although they are not allowed anywhere near the corpse.

Children are protected from incidents that might prove psychologically traumatic to them. Even in adulthood, no one, including my mother, formally told me about my father's death. If I had been told at age four or five, how would I have understood the phenomenon of death, let alone come to terms with the fact that my father was dead. Yes, my father was dead, but there were many other fathers who automatically filled the vacuum left by him.

Death, like God, is self-evident, and society waits until the child grows up to be an adult to understand what death is about. I do not assert that adults fully comprehend the phenomenon of death, but the point is that death is an existential enigma that cannot be explained. Children may be told when someone dies that the deceased has simply travelled and will return soon.

This does not mean that children are not aware of deaths or

divorces, but society tries to minimize their impact on children. I
would be nonsensical to explain divorces to children. In this case, a
in others, children are societal wards and communal responsibility goe
into the care of them. The fact is that children have a world of the
own, while adults have theirs. Children may not even ask what migh
be considered adult questions. For this, they may be reprimanded.

The educated child has a pretty good idea of God as well. Th
notion of God, not necessarily a belief in God, is formed long befor
the enigma of death is confronted. For example, while children at th
period may know the names of God, when asked about the nature c
God they have difficulty responding. They know that God lives i
heaven or the sky— meaning, of course, that God is above and beyonc
the creator of everything, including the sky and the earth.

N o t e s

1. Maynard Mack et al. (eds.), *The Continental Edition of World
    Masterpieces In One Volume,* 3rd ed. (New York: W.W.Norton &
    Company, Inc., 1974), p. 516.
2. Christensen, op. cit., p. 30.
3. Ephirim-Donkor, op. cit., pp. 153-154.

PART III
ADULTHOOD

Chapter 8

ETHICAL EXISTENCE AND GENERATIVITY

When the Akan people conceive of *obra* they have in mind a way of existence in which the individual is morally and ethically concerned with existential issues and their repercussions. But more than ethical existence, obra has to do with generativity (*bo*), hence *obra bo* is ethical existence and generativity. The conception of ethical existence and generativity is intrinsically dualistic. Conceptually, it is not so much contradictory as it is thought of as an *either/or* phenomenon. That is, ethical existence and generativity can be ideal (*pa*) or evil (*bon*). The disposition manifested by an individual is determined by the individual's essential nature (*su*), which, although ideal, can develop into good or evil disposition. However, the individual can alter his or her ethical existence and generativity if it is found to be incongruous with societal ethos.

Furthermore, the double-faceted meaning of ethical existence and generativity finds expression in the way the Akan people categorize the concept into beginning (*ahyese*) and end (*ewiei*). That is to say, that adulthood is comprised of two stages: beginning and end of ethical existence and generativity. It is during the beginning that the individual becomes a social being, bound morally and ethically. The individual begins to grapple with existential issues and their paradoxes. This is a shift from the supervised educational stage where the child is free from moral and ethical responsibilities. The child who has had a difficult educational stage usually welcomes this stage as an opportunity for freedom and independence.

The young adult must exercise discretion as the individual is obliged to adhere to certain ethical principles. Thus, the individual who has begun his or her ethical existence and generativity does so relationally. The married couple, for instance, must know the totemic symbols, taboos and prohibitions, rites, and whatever idiosyncrasies of each other. It means that the beginning of ethical existence and generativity causes some particularly anxious moments. For the first time the individual has to live independent of significant others while fulfilling certain fundamental socio-political duties and observance of protocols.

A paradoxical statement about ethical existence and generativity is that: "The beginning is not the same as the end" (*Obra ahyese ntsede ewiei*). The paradoxical assumption is that the beginning is not difficult, even though it is the most industriously arduous of the two. Here, youthful resilience and energy enable the young adult to work hard and prosper. But, at the same time the lure of opulence may lead to pretentiousness and wastefulness. If judiciousness does not accompany success, one may squander everything by old age and die impecuniously. Therefore, if the young adult who is about to embark on a journey or to be married is told that the beginning of ethical existence and generativity is not like the end, the implied warning is obvious.

This leads to the other side of the equation, the end of ethical existence and generativity. If one accepts the premise that the end is what is necessary or important (*ewiei na ohia*), then does it follow that the end itself is necessarily better? The saying: "You reap what you sow" is applicable here. That is, how one begins ethical existence and generativity has direct bearing on the end. Because ethical existence and generativity is perceived as a journey, only a fool squanders resources before the journey is complete. Such a person is not pitied but scoffed at and referred to as a useless person (*onyimpa gyangyan*). So, the end is used not only in reference to unethical existence in the face of death, but also to mean a change or reversal of fortune for the worse. In light of this, one may say to a person who has squandered his or her wealth: "Is this your end?"

Conceptually, *bo* means to create, to shape or fashion something into whatever form, image, or symbol an individual so chooses. This is perceived as positioning, as the Akan people are very individualistic when it comes to ethical existence and generativity. Contextually, the individualism of this stage may be described symbolically as comprised of two crocodiles joined together in the stomach but vying against each other for food. That is to say that although the Akan are very individualistic in their pursuit of their purpose of being, they do so for the common good of the *ebusua*.

But the concept of *bo* has another meaning that receives little or no treatment, namely, that it can be destructive, evil, or unethical. In this sense it means destroying that which one has created or formed. The point is, ethical existence and generativity can be led creatively and productively or delinquently and destructively. In its larger context ethical living can be ideal or evil.

Ethical existence and generativity is solely an individual phenomenon. Hence the Akan would say: "Ethical existence is an individual endeavor" (*Obra nye woara abo*), because in the end the individual would surely reap the results. Based on this, it would seem to be unfair that the individual be obliged to support his or her matrikin folks. They, after all, have no direct involvement in the person's ethical choices. It must be noted, though, that without the *ebusua* the individual does not exist; moreover, it is the matrikin that nurtures and sustains the individual, offering an identity and meaning that lead to ideal living. Finally, it is often said that: "Ethical existence and generativity is led with patience" (*Obra wotabu bo*). Life cannot be hurried up in order to force the imminence of certain preordained conditions. The person who fails because of an unusually fast life will be told to be patient and let things take their natural pace. However, there are some people who seem to be on a mission to achieve certain things quickly and in the process make mistakes. Indeed, there are people born with such missions, predetermined by their purpose of being. Often the family of such an individual will enquire through divination as to why their ward is so unsettling. This is because to hasten ethical existence and generativity is seen as an invitation to disaster.

What then is the purpose of ethical existence and generativity? Every person wants to know about his or her future, but of course this is not always possible. The goal of ethical existence and generativity is the ideal life as predetermined by one's purpose of being (*nkrabea*). It must be recalled that the *nkrabea* accompanies the soul originating with God as a specially coded existential goal. Therefore, from the teleological standpoint, the goal of ethical existence and generativity is God, when the individual achieves immortality in the esteemed company of the ancestors. The fact that existential purpose is often elusive, ethical existence and generativity may be open-ended; therefore one must strive indefatigably until such time as it becomes physically impossible through death. The termination of life only puts an end to ethical existence and generativity on earth, but the journey motif continues. This is because the Akan people conceive of ethical existence and generativity as a pilgrimage with two phases: the earthly, from Samanadze via conception to death; and the spiritual, from death and return to Samanadze.

But since the individual has no foreknowledge of his or her purpose of being in relation to ethical existence and generativity and God, how can the individual be expected to find and accomplish his or her existential purpose? God has made available all that the individual needs existentially. It is therefore left to the individual to utilize everything that God has provided effectively. If God were to intervene directly, then the individual would not have been morally and ethically responsible for his or her actions. But as it is, the individual has the freedom to make the ethical choices in the pursuit of one's existential purpose. This does not, however, mean that God is aloof. The various rites are God's way of helping those who implore God's help by appealing to the elders who perform the rites pertinent to the ideal life. Ethical existence and generativity is a spiritual quest aided by the rites that make meaning to oneself, the matrikin folks, and the transcendent ancestors and God.

The conceptualization of ethical existence and generativity as a journey makes it a contemplative stage, especially during the latter half of it. Industriously preoccupied, the young adult has little or no time for reflection. At the end, when the body's atrophic phenomenon begins to take its course and when the individual's past actions begin to catch up with him or her, then ethical existence and generativity becomes a critical, reflexive stage. As ostentatiousness and presumptuousness are superseded by meagerness and humility, the individual is obliged to reminisce, wondering what may have gone wrong. My discussants blamed their problems on their youthful indiscretions, witchery, and plain stupidity.

I asked Kofi, a forty-year-old man who was once wealthy but now less fortunate, why things ended this way. Part of his answer was:

> Yes, I had money alright, as you know. But I just don't know what happened to it. The money would disappear from my hands before I knew it. I just don't know how. I would purchase a few things and by the time I realized everything would be gone. At one time I was told by a diviner that I am not supposed to have money. Maybe that is why I lost all my money and even my job, but God is not asleep.[1]

Kofi blamed his financial mismanagement on witchery. It is always easy to shift blame on the elders or some imaginary enemies rather than assume responsibility for one's own ineptness.

Another man, Papa Kojo, whom I met at a bar, accepted responsibility and did not want anyone to pity him. He said:

> I thought of saving for the future all the time, but deferred it each time the thought came up. It doesn't mean I did not save but it wasn't enough. The way my stores were making money I never thought that they will fail, let alone go broke. I had a lot of friends, women. I gave them money but now they see me and pretend as if they do not recognize me. Oh, I had a good time; thank you for the drink, I used to buy for my friends, too.[2]

Uncle Peter lived a few houses away from a relative's house. Through his acquaintance with a rich man, he was made a manager of a cold storage business, the only cold store at this fishing town. The business at the store was voluminous. Within a year or so Uncle Peter put on weight, had a beer in hand always, lavished money on girlfriends, and attended almost every funeral. He ran the business successfully for about three years but started squandering money. This was compounded by the fact that his boss, who lived at Accra, was preoccupied with other businesses there. Uncle Peter was doing splendidly so there was no need for the boss to frequent the store and audit him. One day his boss came to audit Uncle Peter's books and found a lot of irregularities and embezzlement. Moreover, when Uncle Peter could not show anything substantial for the money's use, his boss had no choice but to dismiss him. He died in 1990 after a short illness, probably from drinking.

The reflexivity of ethical existence and generativity does not always connote failure, but it is a time to redirect one's priorities. That is why it is said: "Ethical existence and generativity can be inverted" (*obra wo dan mu*) with the changing of time (*mmbir dze adandan*). If ethical existence could be inverted, then it follows that it could be replenished productively (*obra wogum*). These statements recognize that a particular ethic may not always be right. When one ethic proves unproductive, the individual must realize that one is not bound up to that situation, but is free to try another with the passage of time.

The emphasis put on the beginning is aimed at ensuring a healthy end. Therefore the young adult is advised to eschew unethical existence because the ramifications may revisit the individual in the end. A tenacious beginning is to store up treasure, so to speak, for a more capricious end. So, having led an ideal life and earned the respect and trust of the matrikin, the individual can enjoy the benefits of his or her youthful toils without regret. Such an individual is thought to be wise and judicious. He or she is perceived to have traveled through life's capricious journey with tact, and considered to be the best repository of tradition. Such an individual becomes the embodiment of the ideal life and a symbol of emulation.

When does ethical existence and generativity begin? Adulthood is when a person is faced with existential issues and therefore the beginning of moral and ethical responsibility. For girls, the transition from childhood to adulthood is clearly defined, beginning with their first menses and culminating with overt rites to commemorate the occasion. However, even for girls the start of menses is not the sole determinant of adulthood. Upon attaining adolescent years, children may still remain with their respective families until such time as they are married. Marriage then marks the beginning of ethical concerns because the individual's social perspective widens to encompass those of the other spouse's family. That means the spouse will have to observe certain prohibitions of his or her new family, in addition to those of one's own. Where, formerly, common mistakes and unethical conducts were overlooked, now the young adult will have to recognize them and sometimes go through the discomfort of reproach, often being compelled to make restitution.

At adulthood, men may marry late, but that does not free them morally and ethically. Men may work outside the family as apprentices or may procure government jobs and receive salaries. In the latter case, they are considered mature enough to handle their own affairs. An apprentice, however, does not have the same latitude and fiscal freedom as his salaried and employed counterpart. Like a child under the tutelage of its parents, so is the relationship between the apprentice and his master: the apprentice surrenders all rights to his master. The question of marriage for him may not be considered while the young adult is still an apprentice, unless he was married prior to his apprenticeship. Still, the older an apprentice is the more autonomous he becomes. This autonomy will have its own parameters within the context of apprenticeship's code of ethics. The master, as "parent," has the power to reprimand any of his apprentices, and in extreme cases expel him from the profession. Where the young adult learns his father's profession and actually works with his father, the degree of autonomy depends on the father-son rapport. An obedient son usually rises through the ranks quickly and takes over the entire business when his father reaches old age. Unlike other apprentices, his father may quickly teach him trade secrets and the intricacies pertaining to the profession and may allow him to enter into business negotiations.

Some fathers, however, treat their sons less than kindly in order to demonstrate to others that they are impartial. To avoid having to maintain such a delicate balance between their own children and other apprentices, some fathers tend to send their sons away to their friends to learn from them instead.

I recall that when I left middle school my father (paternal uncle), who was a carpenter, offered to send me away to his best friend to learn carpentry. But I told him I would only learn carpentry if he offered to teach me himself. My presumptuous statement ended the discussion and my hopes of inheriting the family profession.

Between the period boys become men and the time they actually marry, young men exercise semi-autonomous professional freedom.

Their sense of responsibility is tied to their trades, serving as prelude to married life and the ability to provide sustenance and shelter for one's future family. Professional guilds also teach apprentices social, political, and professional codes of ethics, thus preparing them to make the transition to family life.

While boys do not have any rites delineating the transition from childhood to adulthood, girls have puberty or nubility rites3 which, unfortunately, are in decline these days. The reason is usually lack of finances or the encroachment of Western ideas. What I have observed is that where families choose to perform nubility rites, members of a household may pull their resources together and bring several girls together for the rites. A week-long rite I observed included a lame girl of eleven years. I was told by her mother that the girl was under the "legal" age, but due to financial reasons she decided to have her join her three older sisters, ages fourteen through sixteen. In the past such rites were determined by age, but nowadays, it seems, the prime determining factor is economics, hence the decline.

While nubility rites are becoming rare, however, a puberty rite associated with first menses appears to be still prevalent. Sometimes it takes a mother's ingenuity to discover that her daughter has experienced this biological phenomenon in cases where girls conceal their menses. Some of my discussants admit that their discoveries were serendipitous, while others said they became suspicious and confronted their daughters after changes in their demeanor. Although girls are told in general terms to be mindful and report any abnormal passing of blood, no explicit attempts are made to educate girls about their first menses prior to the time they actually experience them. No wonder some conceal their first menses.

Formally, the mark of womanhood is menstruation, and as soon as the matrikin is made aware, the girl is given a sacred meal. This rite is private, carried out without any public pomp. The father may pour a libation and ask the patri-deity for fecundity, guidance, and protection of the new adult member of the family. The father may honor his daughter with gifts of chickens which may be used in feast for the young adult and her friends. This marks the advent of sex education. Her mother or older women from this time on begin with the pedagogical tasks of womanhood, instructing the young woman about the taboos and prohibitions of menstruation, marriage, dietary laws, and societal responsibilities and expectations. Whereas in the past little or no attention has been paid to her movements and activities as a child, her activities will now be circumscribed to prevent her from engaging in dishonorable conducts. From now on her actions have ethical repercussions, so she is advised to be careful in public.

I befriended a young couple at a funeral. The woman was about eighteen and the man was six years older. About two weeks after the funeral I visited them. During our conversation we talked about marriage, death, social responsibility, and a whole array of issues. The wife, Araba, said:

> Oh! I was very apprehensive about marriage, and although my husband and I were seeing each other and took things casually, the very mentioning of marriage and actually seeing his people and my people consummating the marriage made me so anxious. I can recall I did not even want to see him anymore; everything changed all of a sudden. Before I went to him I asked my mother what I should do. I was concerned about my cooking: will he like it, what food does he like and yet I had been cooking with my mother for a long time.
>
> Then I was concerned about my in-laws. You know my father in-law just died; he was nice to me. I asked my mother what I had to do. She told me what is expected of me, including wailing when I went to view the corpse, otherwise, she said, I will bring shame to our family. Because people would always say I couldn't even wail at my in-laws funeral. That part scared me; I hadn't wailed before and even though I had seen my mother cry and sing dirges at funerals I myself have not done that before. I lay all night thinking about it; imaging crying among the many people who will come; Oh, I was afraid. But when he was brought from the mortuary and laid in state Friday night, and I went to view the body I simply did not know how the tears came. I am even ashamed in retrospect. I guess if you have not lost a loved one you really may not understand it.
>
> They say men don't cry, but I saw my husband cry...his father is gone to meet the elders, but I don't believe he is gone....[4]

This excerpt is indicative of individuals at this stage of ethical existence and generativity. Her concerns have to do with relationships and social perspectives.

From what has been explicated thus far, the meaning of ethical existence and generativity is self-evident. I have asked a great many people the simple question: "What is *obra bo*?" Most of my discussants were startled. Some thought that I should have known it, while others questioned my motives. In any event, they would hesitate momentarily as if to reflect on ethical existence and generativity for the first time. The point is, it is a simple pragmatic idea; so near and close, it seems everyone knows about it, but no one, it appears, gives it any serious thought as a concept.

Finally my discussants said: "Ethical existence and generativity is everything a person does in this world" (*Obra bo nye biribiara a onyimpa ye wo wiadzie mu*). Indeed! While the *nkrabea* is fore-ordained and cannot be altered, ethical existence and generativity is the dynamic process of actuating the purpose of being. Thus ethical existence is a generative act as the individual grapples with existential issues from sunrise to sundown. More than being a way of living, ethical existence and generativity is a life-journey, with a beginning, a termination point at death, and a period of accountability before the ancestors.

N o t e s

1. Ephirim-Donkor, op. cit., pp. 166-167.
2. Ibid.
3. See Sarpong, *Girls' Nubility Rites in Ashanti* (Tema: Ghana Publ. Corp., 1977).
4. Ephirim-Donkor, op. cit., pp.174-175.

C h a p t e r   9

T H E   E L D E R S

Is authoritarianism antithetical to free will and therefore an impediment to human ingenuity? Authoritarianism, Wiredu[1] contends, can be a hindrance to free will. He asserts that the Akan society suffers this burden and that the basis for this is:

> ...the principle of unquestioning obedience to superiors, which often meant elders. Hardly any premium was placed on curiosity in those of tender age, or independence of thought in those of more considerable years. Our traditional culture is famous for an abundance of proverbs—those concentrations of practical wisdom which have a marvelous power when quoted at the right moment to clinch a point of argument or reinforce a moral reflection. But it is rare to come across ones which extol the virtues of originality and independence of thought.[2]

Here, it is clear that Wiredu's understanding is flawed. On the one hand, he maintains that the individual is denied free expression of thought because of the elders, an authoritarian group imposing their will on the young and the old. On the other, he affirms a repository of proverbial knowledge in the elders, marked by wisdom. Epistemologically, wisdom cannot be attained without the accrued and successive integration of life's experience. Critical reflection and thoughtfulness develop in the process. It is inconceivable for anyone to be denied the fundamental human right of freedom and yet aspire to embody wisdom, the hallmark of eldership. As resources of wisdom, the elders inculcate in succeeding generations the virtues of humility. From the developmental standpoint, ethical existence and generativity is impossible without first having successively integrated the previous stages. Even a so-called "common" proverb or aphorism must be applied uniquely. The wisdom to apply such knowledge reveals meaning, not dogmatically, but as if for the first time. In itself, it is the product of original thought.

It would be nonsensical for an authoritarian group to be democratic at the same time. This being so, how can the elders be authoritarian when decisions are rendered only after debate? That is, after prolonged deliberations, decisions are reached and handed down to the citizens. Where an impasse exists, a select group of elders are excused to reach verdicts that are accepted unconditionally. Can this democratic process be authoritarian or even exotic? Absolutely not. This process of deliberation and adjudication is quintessential Akan practice and characteristically African.[3]

Furthermore, in light of what has been advanced in the preceding chapters, Wiredu's assertions are indubitably without merit. It has been demonstrated how the parents, especially women, prompted by their belief in the supernatural, attach great importance to conception and prenatal, intrapartal, and neonatal care, until the child is of school age. We have seen examples of the pedagogical methods aimed at enhancing orality and cognitive development. The social and political imperative of this educational stage cannot be overemphasized in an oral society. As Wiredu rightly states with regard to proverbs, the ability to retain countless numbers of proverbs and be able to recall them appropriately to maximize one's effectiveness during deliberation is a process that has its genesis at the educational stage of development.

In addition to cognitive development, children learn the practical side to life by observing and mimicking their parents. Here, the child who is obedient and humble may find favor not only in the sight of his or her teachers but also in that of other friends of his or her primary teachers. This means that the child will have the benefit of being taught the esoterica of whatever profession is being studied ahead of other, disobedient children. In the final analysis, though, it is a process of epistemology through humility and not unquestioning obedience, as Wiredu posits.

Secondly, ethical existence and generativity is possible with or without the educational stage, but, without it, the kind of ethic one would learn would probably lead to delinquency. The rationale behind the educational stage is that one grows up to lead a good ethical life. Even where every effort is put into educating a child, the capriciousness of life is such that one may still end up far short of an ideal life. But with the proper education there is at least the possibility of success in the face of adversity.

The possibility of another chance is allowed in the nature of ethical existence and generativity as a reflexive stage. Moral and ethical reflection is impossible without antecedent experiences. This is why reflection at this stage takes place during the second half of ethical existence and generativity, a stage generally commensurate with eldership. At the onset young adults may be incapable of any serious reflection because they are too busy trying to find their niche in society.

The pedagogical nature of the educational stage includes encouraging attention or curiosity in the youth to enable them to engage in youthful reflection. Moreover, from infancy to wisdom the individual should have led an ideal life ultimately ushering him or her into eldership.

Who are the elders? One response is that Nana Nyame (God) and the *Bosom* are the ultimate elders by virtue of both being addressed as nana. As the *Bosom* makes its monthly cyclical appearances, it renews creation by instilling life and hope in humanity while assuming upon itself the curses, misfortunes, and evils of humanity. Then it dies with them. To ensure the continued survival of humanity the resurrected *Bosom* brings along new life and blessings in the exuberance of food, and in a reciprocal gesture humanity praises the crescent Nana, the Bosom. So the conferral of *nana* on anyone not only means that the individual embodies the essential nature of God and the *Bosom*, but has actually achieved perfection and is worthy of praises and worship. This is exactly the way the Akan perceive their kings to be: divine beings who require the ultimate praise, worship, and sacrifice.

To be an elder the individual must be chosen by his or her matrikin folks. This leader is referred to as *Ebusua panyin* (eldest or head of the matrikin folks). The process begins when older members of that lineage select their candidate and pour a libation (*tsir mpai*) to that effect, among other things. The new *Ebusua panyin* is assisted by the same council of elders who chose him in the governance of his lineage. Together with other lineage heads and sub-kings of a village or town, they constitute the king's council.

Furthermore, there are immigrants who are chosen elders and form part of the council of elders. These may be individuals who have exemplified leadership qualities and have excelled in oratory and wisdom, and in recognition are made elders. These positions may become hereditary. Occasionally, the descendants of these immigrants might contest the kingship. This might be the only time that the descendants may be reminded that their ancestors were immigrants or even slaves. Otherwise, under no circumstance should the origin of anyone be discussed.

There is yet another group of elders. These may be foreigners or philanthropists who have made significant contributions to the development of a community. In recognition of their generosities, these individuals are accorded such honorific titles as "sub-kings" or "militia captains" (*asafohenfo*). All these positions are for life unless an elder chooses to give it up when the appropriate rites are performed. The salient point to remember is that not everyone who bears the title *nana* is an elder, but every elder is a *nana*.

To refer to more than one elder in deliberation the suffix *nom* is added to *nana*, hence *nananom*. A still more definitive name for the elders is *Mpanyinfo*. The term *mpanyinfo*, like *nananom*, is used to refer to a group of elders in conference. In this mode the elders are perceived as a collective body of individuals whose decisions are legal and binding. Individual elders, however, preside over their own affairs. But where a case may involve persons other than their own kin, it is beyond their jurisdiction. Then other elders are called in to constitute a bench before hearing a case.

When two or more elders are seated, the proper designation is *Nananom mpanyinfo*, to refer to an assemblage of distinguished personalities who have converged to address matters of common interest. These personalities may include the king (*Nana Ohen*) and his female counterpart (*Nana Ohenmba*), sub-kings, linguists or orators, militia leaders, heads of the lineages, and pages. Often one may hear the admonition, "The king and his elders are seated" addressed to those who are late, in which case they then hurry shamefacedly to the meeting.

The elders are always thought of as *sitting in state* when deliberating cases. Whether or not the elders are seated is determined by their readiness to proceed with an agenda. Every elder has to take his or her appropriate seat. The seating arrangements may range from unregulated to a more formal, fixed seating. The elder who calls a meeting is entitled to sit at a panoramic seat or point, while the other elders sit on either side of the first in a semicircle. The center must remain unoccupied. Sometimes one may find a bottle of liquor placed on the floor or on a table at the center.

The seating for each royal person is well defined. The king sits at the left hand side of his female counterpart, at the rear and either sides are sub-kings and other elders.[4] The king's linguist or orator (*okyeame*) is always seated in front of the king. These people may form the privy council of the king and therefore constitute a government.[5]

Most meetings are convened before sunrise, allowing the elders to disperse later to their various endeavors. The work ethic of the Akan people is such that all work must be begun before sunrise so that by noon most workers will be resting under the shade of trees. Work reconvenes in late afternoon and lasts until sundown. This work ethic and the notion of time and rest are based on the reading of the solar system. This determines the best times for work.

There is the notion that certain matters cannot be discussed after daybreak. For public and private affairs early mornings are ideal, they receive the largest attendance. Except when the exigency of certain matters calls for afternoon meetings, or when meetings run into afternoon, deliberations are uncommon. Evening meetings may also be called.

Almost invariably prayers are said before proceedings commence. By doing so the participants implore the ancestors to take their honored place in the midst of the elders. Where two or more elders convene, the ancestors are present. The supplicants ask for the ancestor's continued blessing, protection, prosperity, and happiness on the entire community; they offer the reasons why the ancestors have been called upon and pray for the success of the endeavor. A supplicant before praying may lower his cloth (*tam*) to shoulder or waist level with either both or one sandal removed to show respect and humility for the ancestors. The supplicant, however, is never alone; he is always accompanied by another person or an assisting orator to attest to the veracity of whatever is said.

The assistant opens the bottle of liquor, pours some into a cup and drinks it first before pouring and offering to the supplicant a cup of liquor for prayers. Sometimes the supplicant may hold the cup while the assistant touches the tip of the cup with the bottle of liquor three times before pouring the liquor into the cup. Before he prays, the supplicant informs the elders about his intentions. The elders respond by telling him to proceed. The supplicant begins to pray by first acknowledging God by saying: "God, we only show you the drink, but we do not offer you some" (*Nana Nyame, yekyere wo nsa; na yenma wo nsa*)." Then he pours appropriate liquor on the ground as he prays. Never should the liquor be finished before the prayers are done. Whenever the supplicant utters a word, the orator responds by saying: "Yes, true, let your lips flow..." (*Yaa, ampa, woano nko...*). This call-and-response during prayers is also practiced when the king speaks; that is, whenever the king utters any word in public, his orator responds in like manner.

As soon as praying is over, the supplicant is congratulated by those present, who say: *ayeekoo*. The supplicant responds by saying: *yaayie*. Then the assisting orator fills the supplicant's cup with liquor. He drinks and pours the rest on the ground. Then the orator proceeds to share the liquor in the same cup with all present. Even when one does not wish to drink, he or she must taste some and pour the rest on the ground. For kings, however, the liquor may be poured in front of his feet. From one elder to another, all share in the same drink with the ancestors. Finally, the orator partakes of his drink and puts the remainder of the liquor down. Under no circumstance should the bottle of liquor be sealed or emptied at this time. This is to ensure that whoever arrives late will have some to drink.

When everyone has partaken of the drink then the business that brought them together can be addressed. A synopsis of the agenda is offered, after which the orator says to the elders: "Elders, the matter before us is worth considering" (*mpanyinfo yensem pa o*). They respond by saying: "It's well, right" (*oyie*). After a brief pause some may seek clarifications on certain points before engaging in the open discussion.

Chances are that most of those present have been briefed in private but have decided to wait for the proper forum for full disclosure.

If during the discussion a key person enters, then the orator may offer a summary of what is under discussion. Other interested individuals may come in and take their seats quietly without disturbing the proceedings or distracting the audience. They may, however, greet those present before taking their respective places. To offer verbal greetings, the latecomer must ask for the orator and ascertain from him if it is alright to greet the elders. Invariably the answer is in the affirmative. The late arrival then greets the audience: "Elders, I honor your seating" (*mpanyinfo, mema hum atsena ase o*). They then would say: *yaa*. If a king is present, the individual must greet him first before greeting anyone else. To greet the king together with his elders is tantamount to contempt, liable to a fine. The verbal greetings may be followed by handshakes in a counterclockwise manner. When meetings are convened in rooms, most of those who attend must remove their sandals at the entrance to show respect. This practice does not apply to royalty since, in order to preserve their divinity, their feet should not touch the ground.

Discussions can sometimes turn acrimonious and chaotic, especially if it is a public case. Should this happen, there is a way to get the attention of the audience. By custom the elder uses a call-and-response formula. He may say to the audience: "Elders *agoo*," probably more than one time until the audience responds by saying: *Amen*. Or, the elder may say: "Elders, let us unite for order" (*Nananom, homa yenye ko mmfra yie o*), to which they respond by saying: "Let order proceed" (*yie mbra*). This process occurs quite often during funerals when gifts are being presented to the matrikin folks of the deceased.

The *Agoo-Amen* call-and-response is especially employed by musicians. The lead singers in musical groups test the readiness and attentiveness of the overall ensemble by spontaneously and intermittently employing the *Agoo*-and-*Amen* formula. If the back-up singers' improvisation is not up to the desired pitch and tempo, then the lead singer might utilize this formula until the desired levels are achieved. In meetings when order has been restored the officiant proceeds either to say what is on his or her mind or to call on others to voice their opinions. The speaker must be precise, persuasive, articulate, dexterous in oratory, and an adept in customary law and proverbs.

When standing before the elders, the individual must be ready to respond to all questions and be wise enough to decipher proverbs and maxims. Regardless of an individual's ineptitude in such matters, however, everyone is given a chance to speak their mind. Still, fools or anyone who twaddles is shouted down before concluding a speech. Nonetheless everyone has the right to expression, even to the extent of insulting the elders in public. If one chooses to do so, the affront must always be preceded by the phrase "Please" or "With due respect" (*sebi, kafra*), otherwise one is held in contempt and fined.

The goal of the process is consensus. Whether an elder refutes an argument or expresses a differing viewpoint, the goal of all present is to achieve consensus in their final decision. They may not always agree, but when the final verdict is handed down, it is expected that all will abide by it. If there is an impasse, a few of the elders are chosen and excused to go and deliberate while the rest wait. When a decision is reached, they return to report back to the rest of the elders by saying that they have carried out their mandate dutifully. Then their orator announces their verdict and why they arrived at it. This process of deliberation in which select elders hand down their judgment after an impasse is known as *tu-egyina*. Others prefer the euphemism, "consulting with the Old Woman," referring to the primordial woman in the creation myth believed to be all-wise and impartial.

The select adjudicators of an impasse do not always have the final word, however. If they cannot reach a consensus, they return to the waiting elders and upon further consultation may postpone the hearing. This judicial adjournment is called *tu-hyeda*. Occasionally, the situation resolves itself when the parties involved resort to arbitration rather then reappear before the elders. However, the accused, if not satisfied with the verdict, reserves the right to appeal to the divisional or the paramount king of his or her traditional area. But the stakes are quite high for the accused, because more often than not these kings may not overrule their colleagues.

At this time the liquor remaining from the opening of deliberations is now used in closure. The ancestors were invoked prior to the deliberations, and before the meeting ends they have to be dismissed in the same manner. This is effected by pouring another libation, *nsa ase* (dismissal drink). With this final ritual, the orator dismisses the audience. If a king is present, he must rise first before everyone else does so.

The elders are convinced that whenever they convene, the ancestors are in their midst as witnesses. This is to ensure that everything said and done is carried out in spirit and truth. The presence of their eternal counterparts affirm the infallibility of the elders and their verdicts. So, in being dismissed before the meeting ends, the ancestors take with them the verdicts of their earthly counterparts. This ensures that what is legal on earth is also binding in the ancestral world. When finally the deceased appear before the ancestors for accountability and judgment, there would be no room for error.

The elders have a strong moral and ethical conviction to sit in state and settle society's problems and ensure equity for all. This mandate is first entrusted to them by the matrikin folks who turn to them for unprejudiced advice and counsel. Secondly, the elders hold a deep-seated conviction of accountability to their eternal counterparts. The overwhelming sense of accountability among the Akan cannot be overestimated, and if any class of people typify this, it is the elders.

At old age, the elders have transcended their finitude and are living in anticipation of vindication and glorification in immortality, when they shall be judged and found worthy before the ancestors. As depositories of sacred tradition, they look forward to the day when they can give account of themselves to those whose stools and offices they occupy. If found worthy, the newly arrived ancestors are congratulated and rewarded eternally. Hence, the elders do not speak in terms of physical death but rather transformation into ancestors. Consequently, the Akan do not speak of the elders dying. They would only say that the *Nananom* (kings) have gone to the village when they suffer physical death.

But why would the elders or anyone for that matter be accountable when ethical existence and generativity is an individual quest? We must remember that the *purpose of being* or *nkrabea* originates with God. Although individualistic in nature, the purpose of being does not exist in isolation, but in relationship with the matrikin, ancestors, and God. Yes, the child is endowed with its own purpose of being, but it is the community that must prepare and equip the child during the educational stage to enable the child to embark on an ethical existence and generativity that is grounded in and conforms to the matrix of purpose. In daily life the individual is free to make ethical choices. Through education and experience, the individual learns, first, that choices take form in actions that in turn have a much wider effect, rippling outward from the individual through the communal ethos. Secondly, the individual learns that even though all acts have consequences, in most parts only freely chosen acts entail responsibility. The individual thus becomes subordinate to a shared code of ethics and the judgement of superiors. Hence, the individual is accountable to his or her elders, who, in turn are accountable to the ancestors and God.

The elders are active participants in the affairs of their posterity. Actually, older elders claim that they can see the departed ancestors in attendance whenever the elders convene. These older elders have become "children" in preparation for their final homeward journey. Like children, they are now endowed with clairvoyance and other paranormal capabilities. This phenomenon is prevalent among old people, but too often the old experiencing this phenomenon are reviled by youths and spiritually uninspired relatives who attribute their behavior to old age and mental atrophy.

Consequently, the elders take their responsibilities seriously, for they are being watched by the omniscient ancestors before whom they must appear and be judged upon their deaths. The elders therefore stand on the threshold of immortality. In fact, they have already attained immortality or ancestorhood in the flesh and are only awaiting the final transformation through death. Having been elected by their matrikin folks the elders are expected to sagaciously expedite justice. If they fail to execute their duties faithfully they are removed from office having been rejected first by the ancestors and secondly by their matrikin folks. But while infallible before their subjects, the elders are bound by a higher moral and ethical imperative—the ancestors, before whom they must capitulate.

The role of the elders as intercessors is well known. One will always ask an elder to intercede on his or her behalf whenever appearing before another elder. But in going before the elders one does not go empty-handed, but with gifts to propitiate them, knowing full well that the gifts may not guarantee a favorable response. The elders then are perceived as mediators, counsellors, and above all judges. They hold the binary worlds in balance. Balance does not negate contraries, but rather paradoxical axioms are held monistically and orderly at the summit in the persons of the elders, thereby ensuring faith in humanity's continuity. Truth is indivisible; that is, truth is one, but it is collective truth comprised of a body of infallible individuals.

The elders as a body of sages are not apart from, or a class of people above, beyond, and separate[6] from the populace; rather they are a group of sages whose paramount interest is the immaculate transmission of tradition for the preservation of the matrikin and the state.

As archetypes of mediation, they stand between the ancestors, on the one side, and humanity, on the other. No one goes or speaks to the ancestors or God without first going through the elders. The elders intercede on behalf of their communities in order to ensure the continued blessings of the ancestors and of God.

As intermediaries, the elders take upon themselves the ills of society. They are often accused of witchery by their matrikin and blamed for every conceivable mishap suffered by the youth. Consequently, the youth may revile them for difficulties they face as young people, sometimes refusing to give the elders their due respect. Like the *Bosom*, the elders too accept the challenges, knowing that as individuals entrusted with sacred offices, they have aspired to the highest existential office—which, paradoxically, renders them open to the scorn of society. As leaders, they embody socio-political and spiritual power to engender the desired effect on society.

Eldership therefore is a qualitative state of ethical existence and generativity. It is the ideal state of being, achieved after successfully integrating all successive periods of existence. It entails having lived an altruistically ethical life, and bequeathed to the matrikin folks a name that is worthy of remembrance and evocation.

N o t e s

1. K. Wiredu, *Philosophy and an African Culture* (Cambridge: Cambridge Univ. Press, 1980), p. 2.
2. Ibid.
3. Field, *Search for Security*, p. 26.
4. Rattray, *Religion and Art in Ashanti*, p. 133.
5. Busia, *The Position of the Chief in the Modern Political System of Ashanti*, p. 14.
6. Bosman, *A New and Accurate Description of the Coast of Guinea*, p. 132.

Chapter 10

THE ANCESTORS

We have seen in the preceding chapter that the appellation *nana* denotes elder and is utilized in conjunction with *mpanyinfo* to refer to the group of enlightened elders awaiting transformation into ancestors. Also, it has been shown that the *osaman* is a spiritual personality that has undergone somatic mutation after resurrection and is transformed into incorruptible personality. Thus, all those who have undergone these transformations are known collectively as *Nananom Nsamanfo (Asamanfo)*. But while every spiritual personality is a spiritual personality, not every spiritual personality is an ancestor and counted in the company of the *Nananom Nsamanfo* or Ancestors.

To be an ancestor the deceased must first have been an elder, and upon his or her demise become one of the eternal beings. The ancestors are thus a distinct group of eternal saints apart from other spiritual personalities who are also endowed with immortality but are not ancestors.

In chapter eight, ethical existence and generativity as a teleological quest was described as having two phases: the beginning and the end. In the beginning the young adult often finds ethical existence and generativity carelessly liberating and yet difficult, as one begins to grapple with ethical issues. Here is precisely the ethical dictum, that the end is what is really important. In other words, the beginning must be lived in anticipation of the end. The individual must therefore accrue material opulence as well as virtues that are extolled by the matrikin. This is what the individual will be judged by at old age and upon his or her demise.

At old age an elder is apt to reminisce as to whether or not he or she has successfully integrated all successive states of existence. The reflexivity of this period is spurred largely by the imminence of death, the race against time, and accountability before the ancestors. In this way the end has more to do with continual physical and mental atrophy in the face of death. Even though this state is the prelude to a life of immortality, it does not make death any easier to accept by the living. Death, as Nketia states,:

> ...is not regarded as a happy or welcome event. The pathos of mortality and the vanity of some of these beliefs are expressed in some dirges and songs. To be in the hands of Death is to be in the hands of someone indeed! 'If the Departed could send gifts, they would surely send something to their children.' But this does not prevent mourners from saying to the dead: 'Send us something when someone is coming this way.'"[1]

The single most important individual told of any death is the *Ebusua panyin*. As the head of his lineage, one of the responsibilities of the *Ebusua panyin* is informing the king about the loss of his kin with a bottle of liquor. The king might choose to not attend the funeral because he is not to go near a corpse. But if he chooses to attend in the hopes of viewing the corpse, then immediately following the viewing certain purification rites must be performed to ensure his or her continued divinity.

Next, the *Ebusua panyin* convenes an urgent meeting with the elders to discuss the necessary arrangements for interring the body. As you recall, the *ebusua* is a uterine blood group brought together to bury its dead. In light of this definition, the *Ebusua panyin* and his elders dispatch people to inform every matrikin about the loss and when the burial rites will commence. It is the moral, ethical, and civic duty of every adult member to attend the funeral. Where circumstances preclude anyone from attending a funeral in person, his or her share of the funeral debts must be paid nonetheless. The absentee member may be represented by a family member, in which case his or her name is announced during the ritual of debt payments or *nnsawa*.

I happened to be a party to such funeral arrangements several years ago. The corpse was kept at the mortuary for about two months while the matrikin and the dead man's children were contacted. Finally, the date was set for burial. At three o'clock on a Friday morning we gathered at the mortuary. The curious thing was that the women in our group stood outside the gate to the mortuary. Perhaps they were afraid of a dead body, I thought to myself.

Before we retrieved the body, our orator poured a libation. The corpse was then put on a stretcher and carried by four of us. As soon as the gate was opened, the women who I thought were scared proved otherwise: they were outside for a very important function. Spontaneously, they raised their voices in dirges ahead of the men carrying the body. This unsettled me. I had heard and seen women wail and sing dirges many times, but the precipitousness of their wailing at three o'clock in the morning was quite unexpected.

Later I reflected on what their actions meant and what purposes they served. Preceding our party, they announce to the sleeping community and anyone approaching the coming event, their loss and deep sorrow. Likewise, as they make their way home, the wailing marks the direction the corpse is being taken, thus enabling those who may wish to attend the funeral to find the house easily. The dirges also give notice to those who already know about the death and what is expected of them at daybreak. Finally, it serves as the formal beginning of the funeral rites.

In general, the corpse is laid in state all night for wake-keeping, except in cases where decomposition of the corpse has already begun. Such a decomposed body might not be removed from the coffin, let alone be laid in state. When laid in state the corpse is adorned with the best apparel by the deceased's family. Wailing does not begin during the wake until the widow or widower, clothed in black, is brought in by the family of the dead spouse to take his or her seat beside the corpse. Then the wailing begins as mourners file past the body until daybreak.

In the morning the corpse is arrayed with its final apparel and laid in state again for viewing during the day. This may continue until mid-afternoon when the corpse is removed from the bed into its coffin. Here, only close members of the deceased's family or matrikin are allowed into the room. Tensions are always high and chaotic during this time. To see the insane reverence with which a corpse is handled during this anxious period clearly evinces the belief in the after-life.

Nevertheless, the ambivalence toward death is equally evident. On the first instance, the rejection of death in an antagonistic expression of fear and awe does not seem to support the continuity of an after-life. Still, to listen to the dirges and other obsequies that prepare the dead and facilitate safe passage into the ancestral world, one wonders if there is any justification for the repugnance toward death. Of course, death is a loss, and more than any loss it entails deep expression of grief regardless of after-life beliefs held by a people. The dirges I have recorded contain statements like:

> "Why didn't you tell me that you will be going?"
> "Why have you left us this way?"
> "Who must take care of us?"
> "Why are you silent?"
> "Can't you see I am here?"
> "Why have you treated us this way?"
> "Whom did you leave us with?"
> "So you were bidding me bye when you were conversing with me yesterday?"
> "Talk to me?"
> "Oh, death has treated me unkindly."
> "Why me?"

These are the interrogative dirges directed to the corpse while it is laid in state. After this initial state of shock and denial of death, a wave of dirges known as the *nkra* (message) follows. These dirges are positive in that there is acceptance of death. The deceased is about to embark upon the final idealized existence. After death has terminated the first part of ethical existence and generativity, the final journey to the world of immortality begins with the proper burial rites. Realizing this, the wailers begin to send via the spiritual personality of the deceased messages about conditions on earth. The *nkra* dirges include:

"May God go with you."

"Farewell, when you go."

"Go and rest; you are tired."

"Greet all who have preceded us, and tell them we are well."

"Bestow your blessings upon us, and protect us."

"Send us money; we need money to defray your expenses."

"Repay all who caused you harm, and are responsible for your death."

"Go and prepare a place for us."

As you recall, God gives the person to be born *nkrabea* or purpose of being on its descent from heaven into the mundane world. Likewise, the deceased is given *nkra* or messages by the living on its ascension to heaven. This might seem to limit the omniscience and ubiquity of the ancestors. That is, if the ancestors are omniscient why must the spiritual personality be given messages for the ancestors? The answer lies in the fact that the omniscience of the ancestors serves to guard the unadulterated transmission of the messages. Just as no human being can alter an individual's purpose of being, so the deceased cannot alter the message being carried to the ancestors. Like God, the ancestors already know what is being brought. In the same way the soul is the bearer of the purpose of being from God, the spiritual personality is the bearer of the message to the ancestors.

It is imperative that women know how to lament and sing dirges or face social ridicule. I have often heard women quarrelling and sometimes ridiculing one another about the way they lamented at funerals. While pre-adolescent girls might not attend funerals and wail, they still remain close to their mothers whom they observe curiously. With marriage, later, comes certain obligatory responsibilities, including lamentation at funerals.

In general, men (and boys) are not supposed to display any public affectivity and lamentation, though they offer messages to the deceased. I have witnessed some men wail at funerals, but most of these were young. Perhaps the younger the male, the easier it is for him to shed tears. I say this from personal experience because I experienced the same when I lost my daughter. It hit me so hard; I just did not know where the tears and my wailing came from. Later, when I lost other relatives I could not bring myself to break down. I guess I have been hardened through the years after the shock and poignancy resulting from my first encounter with the death of my daughter.

The important thing to remember is that, whatever form the lamentations take, those expressing their grief do so relationally. So one hears wailers referring to the corpse as "Papa"... "Husband"... "Mother"... "Uncle"... "Son"... "Daughter"..."Grandparent"... "Sibling"... "Friend"... "Sister"... or "Brother." The messages take on personal meanings, addressed to the ancestors. The spiritual personality delivers them upon reaching the ancestral world.

The expression of profound grief through dirges follows certain prescribed gesticulations, as succinctly stated by Nketia:

> The singing of the funeral dirges is usually accompanied by gentle and graceful rocking of the body and the head. The mourner turns left for a few paces, then right then left or forward as she likes as if to greet the gathering and thank them for their sympathy or to draw attention to her sorrow and thus earn their sympathy. The arms may be seen clasped across the breast or down in front of the body or held at the sides or at the back or supported on the head—all to convey the anguish of the singer to the gathering. A band or a piece of cloth may be found tied round the body, in the region of the diaphragm— symbolic of anguish as well as a support to the diaphragm and a relief of physical pain.[2]

These gesticulations and dirges, sounding perhaps chaotic to the outsider, combine in words and action to convey over the corpse the mourners' deep sorrow. In lieu of the dirges, the gesticulations communicate the same messages.

It is incumbent on every female who attends the funeral of a matrikin to sing dirges, wail, or communicate by gestures. Those who may arrive later for a funeral (*fun daho*) must perform this rite upon hearing about the death. Upon their arrival they begin at the outskirts of town, wailing and singing dirges as they make their way home,[3] triggering a chaotic collage of dirges from all the women present.

Several days after my sister's funeral, I recall her oldest daughter's arrival. Unaware that she was coming, we heard people wailing at a distance, prompting some of my relatives to wonder if there had been another death in the town. But the wailing grew louder and closer. Suddenly the women who had gathered at the house and those who accompanied my niece to the house converged and burst into a pandemonium of dirges.

Every individual who attends a funeral is rendered unclean and must perform ablution upon their return home. This is especially true of anyone who loses a spouse. The widow or widower is considered unclean by society until such time as certain purification rites (*kuna* and *ayee-gu*) have been performed. For instance, the widow or widower may find it difficult to remarry in the state of impurity because anyone who marries him or her is considered unclean also. In the larger context, the uncleanness is believed to be contagious, affecting the matrikin of the widow or widower. In the case where the widow or widower dies in the state of uncleanness, their bodies may not be brought to the house for burial rites until their corpses have been purified.

Not until the purification rites are performed is the widower or widow free of his or her defunct spouse. Consequently, the *kuna* rite is performed by the dead spouse's family for the living spouse. In this way, the family initiates purification and divorce proceedings on behalf of their defunct kin and so emancipates the widow or widower from all nuptial obligations. When finally the widow is able to perform the *ayee-gu*, she prepares a sumptuous meal and takes it to the dead spouse's family in appreciation for their services. It is only during the final rite that the widow may once again, perhaps after many years, put on ornaments. She dresses extravagantly as she parades before the community. Before this rite she must wear black or darkish cloths only.

The first purification rite may take a week or two for men and up to three months for women. The final rite may take three months to several years, depending on the financial resources of the widow. In general practice, the *ayee-gu* is performed by widows. This discrepancy between widows and widowers in relation to the duration of these rites was brought up by my discussants. Their reasoning had to do with the biological differences between men and women. It takes about three months for any viable pregnancy to be manifested. Thus, if a husband impregnated his wife prior to his demise, for instance, it may take that long for the wife to be certain about her condition.

The Akan have a "levirate" type of practice called *atseow*. The meaning of *atseow* is to spy or watch, and in that sense the widow or widower is being spied upon by the brother or sister of the deceased, who subsequently marries him or her. In the past *atseow* was routine, but nowadays the practice is in oblivion.

The spiritual personality lingers around for forty days. During this time it often reveals itself to some members of its family and vanishes before they make sense of the apparition. On the fortieth day the deceased is mourned and remembered, and on that day or thereafter the spiritual personality departs to the ancestral world.

Because the final phase of the journey to the ancestral world is spiritual, special ritual preparations are made by the matrikin to facilitate the spiritual personality's journey. In the same way that the matrikin nurtured, sustained, and gave meaning to the living, so must it prepare the corpse upon the demise of the person for its final journey to Samanadze.

During the 1970s, I worked as poultry assistant for the Pomadze Poultry Enterprises at Winneba. During the four years or so that I worked there we had a security officer whom we called "Old Man T." He was an elderly man of about 70 years at the time I knew him. Old Man T was a good man because he always made sure that we the youngsters had enough food to eat. As a young worker, at times I would inadvertently go to work without money or without enough food for my lunch. Several of us workers wished to be assigned to his wing so that he might offer us food.

Many wondered about his motivations. Whenever asked, he would only smile. Then one day, as a friend and I were talking with him at lunch, he said: "If you had been to where I have, you would do good." We inquired from him where he had been and so he proceeded to tell us how:

> Everything you do in this world you reap when you die and go to Samanadze, and to do evil is to suffer when you die. And since I have died, gone to Samanadze, and come back to life again I will do good no matter what. When I was young I knew a couple who were always fighting. One day the wife died and strangely enough the husband also died about two weeks later. About a month later I died (although I did not know that I was dead) and found myself travelling on a road. This road was very beautiful and travelled by many people; some going and others coming. I saw people I know and they asked me what I was doing here and that it wasn't my time to travel this road. When they couldn't get me to return they offered me advice on what I should and should not do. They told me not to drink when offered water, not to sit down when asked to, and not to accept and eat any food offered to me.

I continued my journey until I came to a big river and a ferryman who was offered money before he ferried anyone across. When my turn came the man told me that it was not my time to be taken over and besides I had no money, but I insisted. When we arrived at the other side of the river there were also people who were waiting to be brought back, among whom were people I knew and who insisted I return with them, but since I would not return with them they advised me as the others did. Then I came upon a magnificent city. All my life I have not seen any city that is as beautiful as this city. I preceded to the palace and as soon as I got there the people who had gathered turned their eyes towards me and said: 'There he comes, he will tell us what happened.' I went before the elders seated and I told them what happened between the couple, also seated. When I finished speaking I returned, and that was when I woke up only to see people running away. I got down from the bed and started running away, too. That was when I was told that I had been dead for three days and the only thing that prevented the *ebusua* from burying me was my father's delayed arrival from the interior.

I told the *ebusuafo* later I did not die but had only gone to bear witness to the circumstance that led to the deaths of Maame...and Papa.... While I was there I saw people, and there were many, who were suffering because they were very parsimonious when they were on earth. There were some who were hungry and no one would give them food because they never shared, and there were others who had so much that they did not know what to do with them because they gave to people while on earth. This is enough, my children.[4]

Old Man T's post-resurrection story contains all the essentials of what the Akan believe about the ancestral world and the journey there. The dead are buried with pomp. In the coffin are various gifts of money, clothing, and other items of sentimental value. Upon reaching the river, the spiritual personality pays its way with the money or other gifts. Then a ferryman carries it across to the other side.

The ferryman knows everyone he ferries into the mundane for parturition. Likewise, when the individual has completed his or her ethical existence and generativity, he takes it across for the final homeward journey. He not only knows everyone by sight, but exactly when everyone must return to the ancestral world (die). His boat is always full of spiritual personalities who are either being brought into the world or taken out of the world to Samanadze.

If the whole phenomenon of gestation and parturition is a descent from Samanadze to the earth, then death and the ritual preparation of the corpse is an ascent from the earth to the ancestral world. After crossing the river the spiritual personality climbs a ladder called *owu atwer* (death ladder). Like the river, the traffic of spiritual personalities on the death ladder is so voluminous that it gives rise to the saying: "The death ladder is ascended by many" (*owu atwer obako nnfow*). The great number of spiritual personalities constantly descending and ascending the ladder make climbing arduous. The entire journey to Samanadze is so difficult that just before a person dies, water must be given to the dying to facilitate the journey. When circumstances prevent this rite from being performed, the death is believed to be particularly grievous.[5] Finally, when the spiritual personality reaches the ancestral world, it is received.

But where is this ideal world of the ancestors? Samanadze, or better yet the path to the ancestral world, is first below and beneath. The earth must receive the corpse in the same manner the mother brought forth the neonate into the world. It is thus crucial that the corpse be interred. Where circumstances prevent the matrikin folks from locating the corpse, certain rites are enacted to propitiate the spiritual personality to find its way to Samanadze. Or in another instance, where the matrikin folks are unaware that one of their own has died, the spiritual personality of their ward cannot make its ascent. Consequently, it becomes an evil, restless spirit (*sasa*) in limbo, menacing the matrikin folks in their dreams.

Another evidence that the ancestral world is beneath is the fact that libations are poured onto the ground or earth. As we have seen, libations are aimed at offering drinks to the ancestors. The elders always make sure that the ancestors drink first before they partake of their own. Moreover, every elder, indeed all visitors when offered water to drink after a journey or visit, must pour some of the water on the ground for the ancestors. The same ritual is true of every food eaten by the elders.

Secondly, Samanadze is above and beyond. This is because it is a spiritual realm and the abode of the ancestors. Everything tangible is below and beneath, while the intangibles are above and beyond human perception. I have witnessed priests pour libations and upon completion throw the remainder of the liquor up into the sky. When I asked the priests why this was so, they told me that God, the divinities, and the ancestors are above.

The ancestors, like God, are immortal and endowed with omniscience and ubiquity. They could not have such characteristics still buried in the grave and unable to resurrect as spiritual personalities. It is only when the corpse has been interred that the spiritual personality embarks on the homeward journey above and beyond the human realm of tangibility.

The whole conception of the omniscience of the ancestors has its ontological basis in the notion that they are above and beyond. In this way, they overlook and watch over everything in which their descendants are engaged. What better place to have a panoramic view than from up high. Moreover, the invisibility of the ancestors offers them locomotion and omnipresence. Specifically, in pouring a libation, the ground becomes the focal point because that is where they would emerge to take their respective places among humans. The infant spiritual personality, even though it is thought of as originating from the ancestral world above, emerges from below via its physical mother.

The name Samanadze (*Asamando*) itself is illustrative. It points to the location of the ancestral world as above and beyond. The suffix *adze* or *do* denotes a place. This place may be a city, a kingdom, or a world utterly different from this tangible world. Yet, even while different, it is similar to the world of tangibility except that it is the ideal world where the impermanence of the mundane is nonexistent. The only way to gain entry into and become a citizen of this intangible world is by becoming a spiritual personality: hence, Samanadze, the place of the 'saman.

Finally, the ancestral world is within and without, because the location of the ancestral world is an innate phenomenon prevalent wherever the individual is found. For example, when the individual throws a morsel to the ground, the efficacy of the ritual is the same irrespective of where it is performed. More than being an intrinsic quality, it is a shared phenomenon ritualized to convey clearly defined meanings for the individual in relation to the ancestors.

What, then, are the role and responsibilities of the ancestors? We have already established that the elders are sages, counselors, mediators, and ultimately judges. These distinguishing characteristics are immutable upon their deaths. However, they undergo etherealization in concert with their new spiritual personalities and realm of existence. As transformed entities, their essential attributes are the same as their earthly counterparts. The reason for this is that when the spiritual personalities materialize, they do so in the same form and shape, wearing the same identifiable clothing, and engaged in the same work they were known to have done while they were on earth.

The ancestors, having lived, died, and been resurrected and vindicated, have achieved something that no human being has—immortality. They have reached the highest state of existence comparable to God, though not God, because they cannot create or alter the created order. However, they have achieved eternal existence after first achieving perfection as elders. Like their earthly counterparts in relation to the king, the ancestors function in like manner in relation to the ultimate King, God. Yet eternity should not be construed as a finality or a state of stagnation. Rather, it is a dynamically active state due to the phenomenon of reincarnation. It is believed that the ancestors may reincarnate (via their spirits) as many times as possible[6] to help people. Those who die without fulfilling their purpose of being also reincarnate to accomplish their God-given existential purpose.

When the recently arrived spiritual personality gets to Samanadze, it is welcomed, given a stool to sit on, given water to drink, and asked to give account of his or her ethical life. The system of justice is based on aggregation. The ancestors listen carefully and render their decision based on whether or not the spiritual personality before them did more good than evil. If the good outweighs the evil, then it is admitted into ancestorhood. But if found to have done more evil than good, then it is found guilty as a *saman bon* (evil spiritual personality) and membership into ancestorhood is denied it. Thus denied, the evil spiritual personality will reincarnate to undo its evil deeds in the same way a childless couple may reincarnate for the sole purpose of having children. We must understand that the ultimate goal in the world is to lead the ideal life and become an ancestor.

Finally, Samanadze is one spiritual world where every individual originates and where all return. Life on earth is predicated upon the ideal world of the ancestors. There, the ancestors marry and are given in marriage, and children born to their spiritual mothers to constitute the ideal matrikin folks. This is the basis for the earthly *ebusua*.

Akan metaphysics, as we have seen, is such that events in the ancestral world have direct bearing on life in the mundane. In fact, Samanadze takes precedence over the mundane since it is the ideal abode of the infallible Ancestors. It is where the impermanence and inequities of the mundane are made right.

Notes

. Nketia, *Funeral Dirges of the Akan Peoples*, pp. 6-7.
. Nketia, op. cit., p. 9.
. Ibid., p. 17.
. Ephirim-Donkor, op. cit., pp. 209-210.
. Nketia, op. cit., p. 7.
. Sarpong, *Ghana in Retrospect,* p. 23.

Chapter 11

C O N C L U S I O N

.... ❋ ....

The conclusion is also the beginning. We are back again at the ancestral world where it all began, the epigenetic reality of the Akan people. It is here that all metaphysical speculations begin with God, who was, is, and will be, forever (*Odomankoma*)...and the *ebusua*, which was in the beginning with God.

The divine drama that resulted in the death of humanity is yet another expression of God. It demonstrates the distinction between God, as the creator, and humanity, as the created. With the introduction of death also comes two spheres of existence: heaven, characterized by eternity, and the mundane, characterized by impermanence; hence, the quest for perfection (eldership) and immortality (ancestorhood). The question that then arises, "Is perfection and immortality tenable?" is answered with a resounding " yes." That is, the individual is pre-potentiated for precisely that purpose.

As we have seen, to attain oneness with God the individual must undergo a series of developmental stages existentially. Every stage must be verified by the matrikin that confers on the individual commensurate titles. The paramount concern of the matrikin is to ensure an ideal ethical existence and generativity for the individual, leading to perfection and immortality at the ancestral world.

A holistic human being, as we have seen, is the amalgam of complex entities that all work together for the highest good. To be an Akan, the individual must have an Akan mother because she embodies the first developmental stage in becoming a human being. As already demonstrated, any existential discussion has its ontological basis in the blood of the mother. However, blood alone could not constitute a holistic personality. Therefore the Akan people look beyond the mother for the metaphysical entities. Since God is the progenitor of all, the Akan ascribe to God all divine essentials for becoming a person. Furthermore, the father is believed to contribute psychologically to the complete personality in the form of spirit or genetic traits transmitted via his semen during copulation.

The triadic composition of the individual has generated considerable interest in ethnographic research. The views presented here attest to the fact that the Akan have a well-defined conception of the personality that forms the basis for spirituality.

What constitutes the total human economy is the sum of several metaphysical and tangible entities that constitute personhood. In general, these entities are composed of matter or blood (*mogya*), spirit (*sunsum*), and the divine (*okra*). In fact, upon the death of the individual these properties disintegrate, each finding its way to its source of origination.

Birth is the end of existence in the intrauterine, and the beginning of life in the mundane. In recognition of the spiritual origin of the neonate, the community refers to the neonate as a spiritual personality originating from the spiritual world. To become a human being the neonate, known only by its divine or Godly name, is confined for eight days. The evidence of becoming a human being is granted when the neonate is named by its patrikin on the eighth day, thus affirming the father's spiritual rights over his offspring.

In this way the human being is claimed as a communal subject. On the one hand, the individual physically belongs to the mother, from whom citizenship and political rights are inherited, while, on the other, psychological activities—spiritual or otherwise—are attributed to the father. But there is a third aspect that makes life worth living: God. In the form of the soul, Nana Nyame animates an otherwise inanimate being, making possible life in the mundane. To be a triadic but a single holistic being means that life must be lived in a balanced state. In fact, all illness—mental, physical, or spiritual—is thought to be due to asymmetry in the personality. Thus the basis for holistic healing is restoration of equilibrium.

Physically and spiritually, the weak neonate comes under the protection of its mother and father, respectively. In addition to the child's physical development, it is expected that the infant grows spiritually as well. We have seen the nature of the spirit as it manifests itself psychologically. Other attributes of the spirit, though observable, may not be measured in the realm of rationality but approached from the sphere of the religious. As the spirit-shadow travels the world of dreams, it may encounter other spirits more powerful or malign, spirits that may overpower, capture, and even harm a benign spirit. That is, the spirit is thought to be either weak (or "light") or else strong and powerful (or "heavy"), depending on the extent of its development.

From the human standpoint, the father's spirit is heavier or more fully developed than those of his offspring, hence the children must come under the aegis of their fathers. Even so, the children belong to one of twelve esoteric groups associated with the paternal spirituality.

From the Godly standpoint the individual is teleologically pre-potentiated. That is to say that every person is born with a purpose or mission (nkrabea) to be achieved existentially. God is love and the ultimate purpose existentially is achieving the highest love in service to the community and God. In order to achieve the highest existence, good, God has endowed every individual with knowledge that reaches its full potential intellectually as wisdom. The ideal life then is one of selflessness, motivated by a strong sense of purpose and governed by the right moral and ethical choices.

In the same manner that the earthly mother is bonded to her child, the spiritual mother is bonded to every child born to its natural parents. However, the spiritual mother's bonding is fleeting. Despite her efforts to hold on to her children, she soon realizes the futility of her fight as children reach the educational stage.

Prior to consciousness children are endowed with clairvoyance that enables them to maintain close rapport with their spiritual counterparts in the ancestral world. The telepathic capabilities of children, coupled with the notion that they could be the ancestors arriving from the spiritual world, require that children be cared for tenderly.

Although children are endowed at birth with all visual and vital signs, their perception is nonexistent as compared with those of adults. This, then, is the basis for the reflexivity of infants. However, from about six weeks onwards children begin to discern light from darkness and reciprocate when smiled upon.[1] As children develop they become aware of themselves as individuals, autonomously apart from but in relationship with others and the environment. It is during this individuation process that children begin to lose their paranormal capabilities and their link with the spiritual mother. The idea that children are endowed with paranormal capabilities during this period is precisely why the Akan people believe this stage to be spiritual.

With the cessation of all paranormal activities, the stage is now set for the next phase of development, education. In other words, now that children are citizens of the mundane world, they must be inculcated and equipped in the ethos of their new environment if they are to survive and become good citizens.

The educational stage is marked by intellectual development. It is characterized by the ability to comprehend and carry out operations designed to lay the foundation for orality and reasoning.[2] This is a stage of cognitive awareness where the child becomes self-conscious within the context of the community. It is also the period of social awareness when children perceive themselves as a microcosm of a social fabric called the ebusua. From the child's perspective, the educational stage is one of obedience, conformity, and respect for the elders and authority. Consequently, children accept what is taught to them literally, believing in the infallibility of their teachers.

The goal here is to prepare children for adulthood morally and ethically. So from simple tasks to the more complex variables, children soon exhibit mental acuity and dexterity in areas of social, spiritual, economic, and political life. These tasks are designed to lay the foundation for cognitivity, orality, and abstract thinking[3] needed for public life.

The conception of ethical existence and generativity is inherently dualistic as the child's essential nature manifests itself as ideal or evil natured. At the commencement of adulthood, a period coinciding with ethical existence and generativity, the individual is thought to have reached intellectual, biological, emotional, psychological, political, and spiritual maturity sufficiently to embark on a life independent of and yet in covenant with the *ebusua*. This stage is comparable to Fowler's Individuative-Reflective stage because it means that the young adult takes "seriously the burden of responsibility for his or her own commitments, lifestyle, beliefs and attitudes." The notion of ethical existence and generativity, then, is the sum total of one's *nkrabea*. It is an ethical existence and a generativity with a precise period of commencement, accompanied by certain behavioral modifications, a definite period of termination (death), and a final period of accountability before the eternal ancestors.

To prepare young adults for their autonomy and distancing from their matrikin folks, especially for women, certain rites are initiated to raise communal awareness to their new stage. Thus the young adult is ready to embark on ethical existence and generativity. Although autonomous, the young adult is bonded to his or her matrikin for support and renewal.

Ethical existence and generativity has two phases: beginning and end. In the beginning the married or working young adult is expected to lead an ideal life. The pressure to succeed, accentuated by the illusion of youthful elasticity and immortality, may preclude any reflection at this stage. With the advancement of age, ethical existence and generativity becomes reflexive. Towards late thirties and early forties, the mature adult engages in critical reflections. More often than not the individual's worth is measured in comparison with his or her successful peers. The pressure to succeed is intensified by the fact that the adult is always reminded by his or her family about the race against time. The mature adult who successfully masters this stage has already achieved the status of elder, that is, the ability to engage in critical reflection.

The proper way to address the elders is to refer to them as *Nananom Mpanyinfo*. As indicative of their status, they are always thought of as sitting in state when deliberating. Upon assuming their sitting postures, deliberation commences when the transcendent ancestors are implored to their honored place among the elders. Hence, the elders have the power to enforce their adjudications, that are accepted amicably with all amendatory recommendations.

In addition to being judges, the elders mediate between members of their lineages and mend broken relationships, often putting their honor on the line for those who implore their aid. Not only is their intercessory assistance sought to mend damaged relationships, it is also sought when the individual is entreating favor from other elders and the ancestors.

As sages, the elders counsel members of their lineage and anyone who wants their services. They instill in their posterity proper moral and ethical teachings that are imperative to maintaining the delicate balance between the tangible and the spiritual worlds. As counsellors they embody collective truth, assiduously defending the truth in the face of contempt by succeeding generations.

Like the *Bosom* (moon), the elders also embody good and evil as they are blamed for the ills and misfortunes of society by delinquent adults. As a group of infallible individuals who have succeeded in mastering the act of existence, they now await the final consummation of life—immortality. While the corporeal world is fleeting, the reward of immortality is eternal. As elders, they take assurance in their posterity, knowing that they have succeeded in bequeathing to future generations extensions of themselves and names that will be recalled eternally.

We now move from the realm of the mundane to the spiritual for the final stage. The belief in the ancestors is inextricably intertwined with the matrikin. Consciously or unconsciously, no one can gainsay the belief in and worship of the ancestors, as that would negate the reality of the matrikin, which is the mother. The matrikin gives life and meaning to the individual without which the individual is cut off relationally.

To attain the apogee of existence as an ancestor, the individual must first have been an elder. Having attained existential perfection, the elders upon their deaths are ensured a perpetual place in the ancestral world. They are remembered on earth when succeeding generations invoke their names socio-politically and spiritually.

Ethical existence and generativity terminates at death. Yet the journey motif continues after death when the spiritual personality journeys to the ancestral world after forty days. Upon completion, the individual would have completed a cycle: as a spiritual personality (*osaman*), as a human being (*onyimpa-dasanyi*), and again as a spiritual personality (*osaman*). However, the successful completion of the life cycle is contingent upon the divine pronouncement of the ancestors concerning the kind of ethical existence and generativity the spiritual personality led.

The ancestors, like elders, are divine judges before whom the

Akan people must appear and account of themselves. As a community of divine judges they are all-knowing and all-present, watching over the affairs of the world entrusted to the elders.

The relationship between the ideal and earthly matrikin folks is based on the fact that whenever the earthly matrikin folks convene, it must first invoke its heavenly counterparts to be in their midst. Before the ancestors, the elders must show obeisance.

Finally, the ancestors serve to replenish the world by sending those who have never been born as well as those who wish to reincarnate. In so doing they ensure the survival, continuity, and faith in the earthly *ebusua*.

Notes

1. Piaget, *Six Psychological Studies*, pp. 9-10.
2. E. H. Erikson, *A Way of Looking at Things*, ed., Stephen Schlein (New York: W.W. Norton & Co., 1987), pp.604-605.
3. Piaget, *Six Psychological Studies*, p. 63.

GLOSSARY
OF TERMS

Abadai	Beneficence.
Abosom	The seventy-seven Akan deities believed to be the first children of God. They traverse the universe at the behest of God, imbued with ubiquity, immortality, omniscience, and apparitional abilities.
Abrewa na ni mba	A constellation of seven stars that correspond to the seven matrilineal divisions of the Akan people.
Adwen	The brain or knowledge.
Agoo-Amen	The call-and-response formula employed by musicians, orators, and visitors to arouse attention and order.
Ahummobor	Compassion.
Obra Ahyese	The beginning of ethical existence and generativity.
Ahom	Breath or the intangible attestation to the soul in the human being.

Akan people	The nation of peoples found predominately in Ghana and the Ivory Coast. They are bound together by a common theology, language, and ethos.
Asase Efua or Yaa	The names used for the earth as mother.
Atseow	The practice whereby a widow or widower marries the brother or sister of her or his dead spouse.
Ayamhyehye	The burning, churning, or gnawing sensations felt in the stomach triggered by human pathos.
Ayee-gu	The widow's final posthumous rite of purification and severing of nuptial ties with her defunct husband.
Awerekyekyer	The comforting, counseling disposition shown toward the suffering or the bereaved.
Bra (bebra)	Reincarnation.
Ebusua (Nton)	The system of the uterine, consanguineous linear group that converges to bury its dead and share the funeral expenses. They set a date for the final funeral obsequies, appoint a successor for the deceased, and remember the deceased periodically.
Obra Ewiei	The end of ethical existence and generativity.
Fun	An inanimate body, corpse.
Fun daho	The first part of the funeral rite when the corpse is laid in state for viewing.
Krado	The shoulders; seat or place of residence of the soul.
Kuna	The first purification rite performed by the family of the defunct spouse for the widow or widower.
Kyekye per awar	A star believed to be the wife of the crescent moon.
Mogya (bogya)	The blood of the mother that forms the physical component of the person and the basis for the ebusua system of descent.
Nana	King, grand ancestor or parent, and elder. The highest existential state of being.

Nana Nyame	God.
Nananom Mpanyinfo	An assemblage of individual elders who have aspired to the highest socio-political and spiritual office.
Nananom Nsamanfo (Asamanfo)	The community of ancestors in heaven.
NaSaman	The spiritual mother who wills children to the mundane from the ancestral world.
Nkrabea	The esoterically God-given existential purpose.
Nkra	Message or messages sent to the ancestors by the living via the spiritual personality of the deceased.
Nnsawa	The ritual of debts payment during funeral rites by the matrikin folks, friends, and sympathizers.
Nsaman bon	The company of non-ancestral evil beings in heaven.
Nsaman pa	The worthy ancestral beings who constitute the pristine community in heaven.
Ntoro (Egya bosom)	The twelve loosely organized agnatic cultic groups that participate in esoteric rites.
Ntsetsee	The educational stage prior to adulthood.
Nyansa	Wisdom and intelligence.
Obaatan	The beneficent one, God.
Oboadze	Creator, God.
Obra bo	Ethical existence and generativity.
Okra	The soul.
Okyeame	Orator, spokesperson, interpreter, ambassador, and linguist of the king.
Onyimpa Dasanye	A living person.
Onyimpadua	The metaphorical reference to the living person as a tree.
Osaman	The resurrected spiritual personality that supplants the corporeal personality at death.

Otofo	An unusually odd, sudden, and poignant death.
Owu atwir	The ladder ascended and descended by spiritual personalities to and from the ancestral world.
Samanadze	The heavenly abode of the Ancestors.
Sasa	The malign spiritual personality in limbo seeking justice.
Su	The essential nature of the human being.
Suban	The moral character attributes of a person.
Sunsum	Spirit or the genetic character attributes transmitted by a father via his semen to his offspring.
Tu egyina	The process by which a select elders are chosen to render a verdict after an impasse.
Tweduapon	An appellation of God as the ultimate dependable one (tree).
Wer	The inherent will power and energy associated with the heart and the soul.

BIBLIOGRAPHY

Adams III, Hunter H. 1983. African Observers of the Universe: The Sirius Question. *Journal of African Civilization* 5, 1 & 2 (1983):27-46.

Achebe, Chinua. *Things Fall Apart*. New York: McDowell Obolensky, 1959.

Adjaye, Joseph K. Asantehen Agyeman Prempeh I, Asante History and the Historian. *History in Africa* 17 (1990):1-29.

Adu-Andoh, Samuel. *The Sacred in Ghana's Struggle for Justice and Common Identity: The Legacy of Kwame Nkrumah*. Ann Arbor, Mich.: Univ. Microfilm International, 1986.

Anquandah, James. *Rediscovering Ghana's Past*. Accra, Ghana: Sedco Publ. Ltd., 1982.

Antubam, Kofi. *Ghana's Heritage of Culture*. Leipzig: Koehler & Amelang, 1963.

Appiah, Joseph. *Joe Appiah: The Autobiography of an African Patriot*. Westport, Conn.: Greenwood Publ., 1990.

Appiah-Kubi, Kofi. *Man Cures, God Heals*. New York: Friendship Press, 1981.

_____. The Akan Concept of Human Personality. In E.A. Ade

Adegbola, ed., *Traditional Religion in West Africa.* Ibadan: Daystar Press, 1987:259-264.

Arhin, Kwame. A Note on the Asante Akonkofo: A Non-literate Subelite, 1900-1930. *Africa* 56, 1 (1986):25-31.

_____. The Political and Military Roles of Akan Women. In C. Oppong, ed., *Female and Male in West Africa.* London: George Allen & Unwin, 1983:91-98.

_____. Rank and Class Among the Asante and Fante in the Nineteenth Century. *Africa* 53, 1 (1983):2-22.

Augustine, St. *The City of God.* Trans. by M. Dodds. New York: The Modern Library, 1950.

_____. *The Confessions.* Trans. by J.K. Ryan. Garden City: Doubleday & Co., 1960.

Bartle, Philip I.W. Forty Days: The Akan Calendar. *Africa* 48, 1 (1978): 80-84.

Bascom, William R. and Herskovits, Melville J., eds., *Continuity and Change in African Cultures.* Chicago: Univ. of Chicago Press, 1959.

Bastide, Roger. *African Civilization in the New World.* Trans. by Peter Green. London: C. Hurst & Co., 1971.

_____. *The African Religions of Brazil.* Baltimore: Johns Hopkins Univ. Press, 1978.

Bay, Edna G., ed. *Women and Work in Africa.* Boulder, Colo.: Westview Press, 1982.

Beecham, John. *Ashantee and the Gold Coast.* London: Dawsons of Pall Mall, 1968.

Beltis, Joseph D., ed. *Phenomenology of Religion: Eight Modern Descriptions of the Essence of Religion.* London: SCM Press Ltd., 1969.

Bernal, Martin. *Black Athena: The Afroasiatic Roots of Classical Civilization.* Vol. I. New Brunswick: Rutgers Univ. Press, 1987.

Blazer, Doris A., ed. *Faith Development in Early Childhood.* Kansas City: Sheed & Ward, 1989.

Bleek, Wolf. The Value of Children to Parents in Kwahu, Ghana. In Christine Oppong et al., eds., *Marriage, Fertility and Parenthood in West Africa.* Canberra: Australian Natl. Univ., 1978:307-329.

_____. Did the Akan Resort to Abortion in Pre-colonial Ghana? *Africa* 60, 1 (1990):121-131.

Boahen, Adu. *Ghana: Evolution and Change in the Nineteenth and Twentieth Centuries*. London: Longman Group Ltd., 1975.

_____. *Topics in West Africa*. 2nd ed. London: Longman Group Ltd, 1966.

Bosman, William [1704]. *A New and Accurate Description of the Coast of Guinea*. New York: Barnes & Nobles, 1967.

Bowdich, T. Edward. *Mission from Cape Coast Castle to Ashantee, with a Descriptive Account of that Kingdom*. London: Griffith & Garran, 1773.

Breidenbach, Paul S. Colour Symbolism and Ideology in Ghanaian Healing Movement *Africa* 46, 2 (1976):137-145.

Brown, Peter. *Augustine of Hippo*. Berkeley/Los Angeles, Calif.: Univ. of California Press, 1969.

Budge, E.A. Wallis. *The Egyptian Book of the Dead*. New York: Dover, 1967.

Busia, K.A. *The Position of the Chief in the Modern Political System of Ashanti*. London: Oxford Univ. Press, 1951.

_____. The Ashanti. In Daryll Forde, ed., *African Worlds: Studies in the Cosmological Ideas and Social Values of African Peoples*. London: Oxford Univ. Press, 1954:190-209.

Christaller, J.G. *Dictionary of the Asante and Fante Language Called Tshi (Twi)*. 2nd ed. Basel: Evangelical Missionary Society, 1933.

Christensen, James Boyd. The Adaptive Functions of Fanti Priesthood. In William Bascom and Melville Herskovitz, ed., *Continuity and Change in African Culture*. Chicago: Univ. of Chicago Press, 1959:257-278.

_____. *Double Descent Among the Fanti*. New Haven: Human Relations Area Files, 1954.

Christian, Angela. *Adinkra Oration*. Accra: Catholic Book Centre, 1976.

Chukwukere, I. Akan Theory of Conception—Are the Fante Really Aberrant? *Africa* 48, 2 (1978): 135-148.

_____. Agnatic and Uterine Relations Among the Fante: Male/Female Dualism. *Africa* 52, 1 (1982): 61-68.

Claridge, Walton W. [1951] *A History of the Gold Coast and Ashanti: From the Earliest Times to the Commencement of the Twentieth Century*. 2 vols. New York: Barnes & Noble, 1964.

Cole, Herbert M. and Ross, Doran H. *The Arts of Ghana*. Los Angeles: Univ. of California, 1977.

Crim, Keith; Bullard, Roger A.; and Shinn, Larry D., eds. *Abingdon Dictionary of Living Religions*. Nashville: Abingdon, 1981.

Cudjoe, Selwyn R. Kwame Nkrumah: The Man and His World. In I.V. Sertima, ed., *Great Black Leaders*. New Haven: Journal of African Civilizations Ltd., 1988:322-345.

Da Mota, A. Teixeira and Hair, P.E.H. *East of Mina: Afro-european Relations on the Gold Coast in the 1550 and 1560s, An Essay with Supporting Documents*. Madison: Univ. of Wisconsin, 1988.

Damuah, Vincent K. *The Changing Perspective of Wasa Amanfi Tradition Religion in Contemporary Africa*. High Wycomb, England: Univ. Microfilm Ltd, 1971.

Danquah, J.B. *The Akan Doctrine of God*. London: Frank Cass & Co., Ltd., 1968.

Davidson, Basil. *The African Genius*. Boston/Toronto: Little, Brown & Co., 1969.

_____. *The Lost Cities of Africa*. Boston/Toronto: Little, Brown & Co., 1979.

Davidson, Basil, with Buah, F.K. *A History of West Africa, 1000-1800*. London: Longman, 1977.

deGraft-Johnson, J.C. *African Glory*. Baltimore: Black Classics Press, 1986.

de Marees, Pieter [1602]. *Description and Historical Account of the Gold Kingdom of Guinea (1602)*. Trans. & ed., Albert van Dntzig & Adam Jones, Oxford: Oxford Univ. Press, 1987.

Diop, Cheika Anta. *The African Origin of Civilization: Myth or Reality*. West Point: Lawrence Hill & Co., 1974.

_____. Origin of the Ancient Egyptians. *Journal of African Civilizations* 8, 1 (1986):35-63.

Dykstra, Craig and Parks, Sharon, eds., *Faith Development and Fowler*. Birmingham, Ala.: Religious Education Press, 1986.

Eliade, Mircea. *The Sacred and the Profane: The Nature of Religion*. New York/London: Harcourt Brace Jovanovich, 1959.

_____. *Myth and Reality*. Trans. by Williard R. Trask. New York: Harper and Row, 1963.

_____. *Rites and Symbols of Initiation: The Mysteries of Birth and Rebirth*. Trans. by Willard R. Trask. New York: Harper & Row, 1958.

Ellis, A.G. *The Tshi-speaking Peoples of the Gold Coast of West Africa*. London: Chapman & Hall, Ltd, 1887.

Ephirim-Donkor, Anthony S. *African Personality and Spirituality: The Akanfo Quest for Perfection and Immortality*. Ann Arbor, Michigan: Univ. Microfilms, 1994.

Erikson, Erik H. *A Way of Looking at Things*. Ed., Stephen Schlein. New York: W.W. Norton & Co., 1987.

_____. *Ghandi's Truth*. New York: W.W. Norton & Co., 1969.

_____. *Identity, Youth, and Crisis*. New York: W.W. Norton & Co., 1968.

_____. *Insight and Responsibility*. New York: W. W. Norton & Co., 1964.

_____. *The Life Cycle Completed*. New York: W.W. Norton & Co., 1982.

_____. *Young Man Luther*. New York: W.W. Norton & Co., 1958

Etienna, Mona. Gender Relations and Conjugality Among the Baule. In Christine Oppong et al., eds., *Marriage, Fertility and Parenthood in West Africa*. Canberra: Australia Natl. Univ., 1978:303-319.

Evans-Pritchard, E. E. *Witchcraft, Oracles and Magic Among the Azande*. London: Oxford Univ. Press, 1937.

_____. *Nuer Religion*. London: Oxford Univ. Press, 1956.

Fiawood, D.K. Some Patterns of Foster Care in Ghana. In Christine Oppong et al., eds., *Marriage, Fertility and Parenthood in West Africa*. Canberra: Australia Natl. Univ., 1978:273-288.

Field, M.J. *Akim-Kotoku: An Oman of the Gold Coast*. London: The Crown Agents for the Colonies, 1948.

_____. *Search for Security: An Ethno-psychiatric Study of Rural Ghana*. London: Faber & Faber, 1960.

_____. *Social Organization of the Ga People*. London: The Crown Agents for the Colonies, 1940.

Fischer, Louis. *Ghandi: His Life and Message for the World*. New York: New American Library, 1954.

Forde, Daryll, ed. *African Worlds: Studies in the Cosmological Ideas and Social Values of African Peoples.* London: Oxford Univ. Press, 1954.

Fowler, James W. *Becoming Adult, Becoming Christian: Adult Development and Christian Faith.* San Francisco: Harper & Row, 1984.

_____. *Faith Development and Pastoral Care.* Philadelphia: Fortress Press, 1987.

_____. Faith and the Structure of Meaning. In Craig Dykstra and Sharon Parks, eds., *Faith Development and Fowler.* Birmingham, Ala.: Religious Education Press, 1986:15-42.

_____. John Wesley's Development of Faith. In M. Douglas Meeks, ed., *The Future of the Methodist Theological Tradition.* Nashville: Abingdon, 1985:172-208.

_____. *Stages of Faith: The Psychology of Human Development and the Quest for Meaning.* San Francisco: Harper & Row, 1981.

_____. Stages of Faith and Adults' Life Cycles. In Kenneth Stokes, ed., *Faith Development in the Adult Life Cycle.* New York: Sadlier, 1983:179-207.

_____. Strength for the Journey: Early Childhood Development in Selfhood and Faith. In Doris Blazer, ed., *Faith Development in Early Childhood.* Kansas City: Sheed & Ward, 1989:1-36.

Freud, Sigmund. *An Outline of Psycho-analysis.* Trans. & ed., James Strachey. New York: W. W. Norton & Co., 1969.

_____. *General Psychological Theory.* New York: Macmillan Publ. Co., 1963.

_____. *Inhibitions, Symptoms and Anxiety.* Trans. by Alix Strachey and James Strachey. New York: W.W. Norton & Co., 1959.

_____. *On Dreams.* Trans. by. James Strachey. New York: W. W. Norton & Co., 1952.

_____. *Sexuality and the Psychology of Love.* New York: Macmillan Publ. Co., 1963.

_____. *Civilization and its Discontents.* Trans. & ed., James Strachey. New York: W.W. Norton & Co., 1961.

_____. *The Sexual Enlightenment of Children.* New York: Macmillan Publ. Co., 1963.

Fried, Martha N., and Fried, Morton H. *Transitions: Four Rituals in Eight Cultures.* New York: Penguin Books, 1980.

Fynn, J.K. *Asante and its Neighbors, 1700-1897.* London: Longman Group Ltd, 1971.

Garlake, P. *Great Zimbabwe.* New York: Stein & Day, 1973.

Gilbert, Michelle. The Sudden Death of a Millionaire: Conversion and Consensus in a Ghanaian Kingdom. *Africa* 58, 3 (1988): 291-313.

Gilligan, Carol. *In a Different Voice: Psychological Theory and Women's Development.* Cambridge, Mass: Harvard Univ. Press, 1981.

Goody, Jack. Ethnohistory and the Akan of Ghana. *Africa* xxix, 1 (1959): 67-81.

_____. *The Domestication of the Savage Mind.* Cambridge: Cambridge Univ. Press, 1977.

Griaule, Marcel. The Idea of Person Among the Dogon. In Simon and Phoebe Ottenberg, eds., *Cultures and Societies of Africa.* New York: Random House, 1960:365-371.

Griaule, Marcel and Dieterlen, Germaine. The Dogon. In Daryle Forde, ed., *African Worlds: Studies in the Cosmological Ideas and Social Values of African Peoples.* London: Oxford Univ. Press, 1954:83-110.

Gyekye, Kwame. *An Essay on African Philosophical Thought: The Akan Conceptual Scheme.* Cambridge: Cambridge Univ. Press, 1987.

Hagan, George P. Marriage, Divorce and Polygyny in Winneba. In Christine Oppong, ed., *Female and Male in West Africa.* London: George Allen & Unwin, 1983:192-203.

Herodotus. *The History.* Trans. by David Green. Chicago: The Univ. of Chicago Press, 1987.

Huber, Hugo. *The Krobo: Traditional, Social and Religious Life of a West African People.* St. Augustine near Bonn: Anthropos Institute, 1963.

Huizer, Gerrit, and Mannheim, Bruce, eds. *The Politics of Anthropology: From Colonialism and Sexism Toward a View from Below.* The Hague: Monton Publ., 1979.

Idowu, E. Bolaji. *African Traditional Religion: A Definition.* New York: Orbis Books, 1973.

Johannson, Donald C. and Edey, Martland. *Lucy: The Beginning of Humankind.* New York: Simon & Schuster, 1981.

Jones, Reginal L., ed. *Black Adult Development and Aging.* Berkeley, Calif: Cobb & Henry, Publ., 1989.

Jung. C.G., *Answer to Job*, 2nd Vol. Trans. by R.F.C. Hull. Princeton, N.J.: Princeton Univ. Press, 1973.

_____. *Memories, Dreams, Reflections*. Trans. by Richard Winston and Clara Winston. New York: Vintage Books, 1965.

_____. *Psyche and Symbol*. ed., Violet S. de Laszle. Garden City, N.Y.: Doubleday & Co., Inc., 1958.

_____. *Psychology and Religion*. New Haven: Yale Univ. Press, 1938.

_____. *Symbols of Transformation*. Vol. 5. Trans. by R.F.G. Hull. Princeton, N.J.: Princeton Univ. Press, 1976.

Kellner, Douglas. *Kwame Nkrumah*. New York: Chelsea House, 1987.

Kenyatta, Jomo. *Facing Mt. Kenya*. London: Secker & Warburg, 1961.

Kierkegaard, Soren. *Fear and Trembling: Repetition*. Trans. by Howard Hong and Edna Hong. Princeton, N.J.: Princeton Univ. Press, 1983.

_____. *Either/Or*. Vol. I. Trans. By David F. Swanson and Lillian Swanson. Princeton, N.J.: Princeton Univ. Press, 1959.

_____. *The Sickness Unto Death*. Trans. & ed., Howard Hong and Edna Hong. Princeton, N.J.: Princeton Univ. Press, 1980.

_____. *Works of Love*. Trans & ed., Howard Hong and Edna Hong. New York: Harper & Row, 1962.

Kohlberg, Lawrence. *Essays on Moral Development: The Psychology of Moral Development*, Vol. I. New York: Harper & Row, 1984.

_____. My Personal Search for Universal Morality. *Moral Education Forum* 11, 1 (1986): 4-10.

LaFontaine, J.S. *Initiation: Ritual Drama and Secret Knowledge Across the World*. Manchester: Manchester Univ. Press, 1986.

Lau, D.C., trans & intro. 1979. *Confucius: The Analects*. Middlesex, England: Penguin Books, 1979.

Laye, Camara. *The Dark Child: An Autobiography of an African Boy*. Farrar, N.Y.: Straus & Giroux, 1981.

Leacock, Seth and Leacock, Ruth. *Spirits of the Deep: A Study of an Afro-Brazilian Cult*. Garden City, N.Y.: Doubleday & National History Press, 1972.

Leakey, Mary. *Disclosing the Past*. New York: Doubleday & Co., 1984.

LeVine, Robert A. Patterns of Personality in Africa. *Ethos* 1, 2 (1973): 123-152.

Lucas, J. Olumide. *The Religion of the Yorubas*. Lagos: C.M.S. Bookstore, 1948.

Lystad, Robert A. *The Ashanti: A Proud People*. New Brunswick, N.J.: Rutgers Univ. Press, 1958.

_____. Marriage and Kinship Among the Ashanti and the Agni: A Study of Differential Acculturation. In William Bascom and Melville Herskovits, eds., *Continuity and Change in African Cultures*. Chicago: Univ. of Chicago Press, 1959:187-204.

Lystad, Mary H. Paintings of Ghanaian Children. *Africa* xxx, 3 (1960): 238-242.

Mack, Maynard et al, eds. *The Continental Edition of World Masterpieces*. 3rd ed. New York: W.W.Norton & Company, 1974.

Makepeace, Margaret. English Traders on the Gold Coast, 1657-1668: An Analysis of the East Indian Company Archive. *History in Africa* 16 (1989): 237-284.

Mandela, Winnie. *Part of My Soul Went With Him*. New York: W.W. Norton & Co., 1985.

Mbiti, John. *African Religion and Philosophy*. Garden City, N.Y.: Anchor Books, 1969.

McCaskie, T.C. Accumulation, Wealth and Belief in Asante History, 1. to the Close of the Nineteenth Century, *Africa* 53, 1 (1983): 23-43.

Melvin, Harold Wesley, Jr. *Religion in Brazil: A Sociological Approach to Religion and its Integrative Function in Rural-Urban Migrant Adjustment*. London: Univ. Microfilms International, 1970.

Meredith, Henry [1812]. *An Account of the Gold Coast of Africa: With a Brief History of the African Company*. London: Frank Cass & Co., Ltd., 1976

Meyerowitz, Eva L.R. *The Akan of Ghana*. London: Faber & Faber, Ltd., 1958.

Mikell, Gwendolyn. Filiation, Economic Crisis and the Status of Women in Rural Ghana. *Canadian Journal of African Studies* 18, 1 (1984):195-218.

Miller, Alice. *Thou Shalt Not Be Aware: Society's Betrayal of the Child*. Trans. by Hildegrade and Hunter Hannun. New York: Farrar Straus Giroux, 1984.

Mitchell, Juliet, ed. *The Selected Melanie Klein*. New York: The Free Press, 1987.

Mitchell, Henry W. *Black Belief: Folk Beliefs of Blacks in America and West Africa*. New York: Harper & Row, 1975.

Mitchell, Robert Cameron. *African Primal Religion*. Niles, Ill.: Argus Comm., 1977.

Nahler, Margaret S., Fred Pine, Anni Bergman. 1975. *The Psychological Birth of the Human Infant: Symbiosis and Individuation*. New York: Basic Books, 1975.

Niane, D.T. [1963]. *Sundiata: An Eic of Old Mali*. Trans. by Pickett. London: Longman Group Ltd.,1973.

Niebuhr, H. Richard. 1941. *The Maning of Revelation*. New York: Macmillan Publ. Co., 1941.

_____. *Radical Monotheism and Western Culture: With Supplementary Essays*. New York: Harper & Row, 1943.

Nketia, J.H. *Funeral Dirges of the Akan*. Ghana: Achimota, 1955.

Oates, Stephen B. *Let the Trumpet Sound: The Life of Martin Luther King, Jr*. New York: Harper & Row, 1982.

Oduyoye, Modupe. Man's Self and its Spiritual Double. In E.A. Ade Adegbola, ed., *Traditional Religion in West Africa*. Ibadon: Daystar Press, 1983:273-288.

_____. Festivals: The Cultivation of Nature and the Celebration of History. In E.A. Ade Adegbola, ed. *Traditional Religion in West Africa*. Ibadan: Daystar Press, 1983: 150-169.

Okali, Christine. *Cocoa and Kinship in Ghana: The Matrilineal Akan of Ghana*. London: Keagan Paul, Int., 1983.

Opoku, Kofi A. *West African Traditional Religion*. Accra: FEP Int. Private Ltd., 1978.

Oppong, Christine, ed. *Female and Male in West Africa*. London: George Allen & Unwin, 1983.

_____. *Marriage Among Matrilineal Elite*. London: Cambridge Univ. Press, 1974.

Oppong, Christine; Abada, G.; Bekombo-Priso, M.; and Nogey, J., eds. *Marriage, Fertility and Parenthood in West Africa*, 4, 1&2. Canberra: Australian Natl. Univ., 1978.

Oppong, Christine and Bleek, Wolf. Economic Models and Having Children: Some Evidence from Kwahu, Ghana. *Africa* 52, 4 (1982):15-33.

Oppong, Christine; Okali, Christine; and Houghton, Beverley. Women Power: Retrograde Steps in Ghana. *The African Studies Review* XVIII, 3 (1974):71-84.

Ottenberg, Phoebe V. The Changing Economic Position of Women Among the Afikpo Ibo. In William R. Bascom and Melville Herskovits, eds. *Continuity and Change in African Cultures.* Chicago: The Univ. of Chicago Press, 1959:205-223.

Ottenberg, Simon. *Boyhood Rituals in an African Society: An Interpretation.* Seattle: Univ. of Washington Press, 1989.

Ousmane, Sembene. *God's Bits of Wood.* Trans. by Francis Price. London: Heinemann, 1988.

Parin, Paul; Morgenthaler, Fritz; and Parin-Matthéy Goldy. *Fear Thy Neighbor As Thyself: Psychoanalysis and Society Among the Anyi of West Africa.* Trans. by Patricia Klamerth. Chicago & London: Univ. of Chicago Press, 1980.

Parrinder, Geoffrey. *African Traditional Religion.* Westport, Conn: Greenwood Press, 1976.

_____. *West African Religion: A Study of the Belief and Practices of Akan, Ewe, Yoruba, Ibo and Kindred Peoples.* London: Epworth Press, 1969.

Paul, Robert A. Symbolic Interpretation in Psychoanalysis and Anthropology. *Ethos* 8, 4 (1990):286-294.

_____. *The Tibetan Symbolic World: Psychoanalytic Explorations.* Chicago/London: Univ. of Chicago Press, 1982.

Piaget, Jean. *The Child and Reality: Problems of Genetic Psychology.* Trans. by Arnold Rosin. New York: Grossman, 1973.

_____. *The Moral Judgment of the Child.* Trans. by Marjorie Gabain. New York: The Free Press Macmillan, 1965.

_____. *Six Psychological Studies.* Trans. by Anita Tenzer. New York: Vintage Books, 1967.

Raboteau, Albert J. *Slave Religion: The "Invisible Institute" in the Antebellum South.* Oxford: Oxford Univ. Press, 1980.

Radhakrishnan, Sarvepalli, and Moore, Charles A., eds. *A Sourcebook in Indian Philosophy.* Princeton, N.J.: Princeton Univ. Press, 1957.

Rattray, R.S. *Ashanti.* Oxford: At The Clarendon Press, 1923.

_____. *Religion & Art in Ashanti.* Oxford: At the Clarendon Press, 1927.

Ray, Benjamin C. *African Religions: Symbol, Ritual, and Community.* Englewood Cliffs, N.J.: Prentice-Hall, 1976.

Reimer, Joseph; Paolitto, Diana Pritchard; and Hersh, Richard H. *Promoting Moral Growth: From Piaget to Kohlberg.* London: Longman, 1983.

Reindorf, J., comp. *Scandinavians in Africa: Guide to Materials Relating to Ghana in Danish Archives.* Oslo: Universitets Forlaget, 1980.

Riesmann, Paul. The Person and the Life Cycle in African Social Life and Thought. *African Studies Review* 29, 2 (1986):71-138.

Sarpong, Peter. *Ghana in Retrospect: Some Aspects of Ghanaian Culture.* Tema: Ghana Publ. Corp., 1974.

_____. *Girls' Nubility Rites in Ashanti.* Tema: Ghana Publ. Corp., 1977.

Sertima, Ivan V., ed. *Great Black Leaders: Ancient and Modern.* New Haven: Journal of African Civilizations Ltd., Inc., 1988.

Smith, Edwin W., ed. *African Ideas of God.* London: Edinburgh House Press, 1950.

_____. *The Golden Stool.* Garden City, N.Y.: Doubleday, Doran & Co., 1928.

Soyinka, Wole. *The Interpreters.* London: Heinemann, 1965.

Talbot, P.A. *Some Nigerian Fertility Cults.* New York: Barnes & Nobles, 1969.

Thiong'o, wa Ngugi. *A Grain of Wheat* Rev. ed. London: Heinemann, 1967.

Tillich, Paul. *Dynamics of Faith* Vol. 10. ed., Ruth N. Anshen. New York: Harper & Brothers, 1957.

Turnbull, Colin M. *The Human Cycle.* New York: Simon and Schuster, 1983.

_____. *The Forest People.* New York: Simon and Schuster, 1967.

Turner, Victor. *Dramas, Fields and Metaphors: Symbolic Action in Human Society.* Ithaca, N.Y.: Cornell Univ. Press, 1974.

_____. *The Forest of Symbols: Aspects of Ndembu Ritual.* New York: Cornell Univ. Press, 1967.

_____. *The Ritual Process: Structure and Anti-structure.* Ithaca, N.Y.: Cornell Univ. Press, 1977.

Vansina, Jan. *Oral Tradition: A study in Historical Methodology.* Trans. by H.M. Wright. Chicago: Aldine Publ., 1965

Walker, L. Cognitive and Perspective-taking Prerequisites for Moral Development. *Child Development* 51 (1980):131-139.

Ward, W.E.F. *A History of the Gold Coast*. London: George Allen & Unwin Ltd, 1948.

Wilks, Ivor. Akwamau and Otublohum: An Eighteenth-Century Akan Marriage Arrangement. *Africa* xxix, 4 (1959):391-404.

_____. *Asante in the Nineteenth Century: The Structure and Evolution of a Political Order*. London: Cambridge Univ. Press, 1957.

Winnicott, D.W. *Playing & Reality*. New York: Routledge, 1989.

Wiredu, Kwasi. *Philosophy and an African Culture*. Cambridge: Cambridge Univ. Press, 1980.

Wright, Jr. J. Eugene. *Erikson: Identity and Religion*. New York: The Seabury Press, 1984.

Wyllie, Robert W. The Aboakyer of the Effutu: A Critique of Meyerowitz's Account. *Africa* xxxvii,1 (1967):81-85.

Yarak, Larry W. Elmina and Greater Asante in the Nineteenth Century. *Africa* 56, 1 (1986):33-52.

Zuesse, Even M. *Ritual Cosmos: The Sanctification of Life in African Religions*. Athens, Ohio: Ohio Univ. Press, 1979.

INDEX

37-38, 41-42, 45, 59-62,
65, 84, 125, 132, 134,
136-139, 141, 143-145,
148
Antubam, Kofi, 21, 35
Anxiety, 40, 42, 45
Apparition, 14, 32, 59, 136
Apparitions, 61, 63
Appearance, 32, 35
Appellation, 129
Appiah-Kubi, Kofi, 21, 74
Apprentices, 113-114
Arbitration, 124
Archetypal
    models, 30
    community, 4-5, 8, 30,
        33-34, 51-52, 54, 65-67,
        75, 120-121, 125, 131,
        135, 144-146, 149
    symbol, 30, 33, 59, 65,
        109, 112
    mother, 8, 15-18, 20-24,
        32-34, 37-40, 42-47, 50,
        56, 62, 67, 74, 83-88,
        94, 97, 99-100, 103,
        114-115, 134, 138-139,
        144-146, 148
Archetypes, 127
Artistic expressions
    skills, 93, 97-98, 102
Asabu Amanfi, 30
Asante, 6, 9, 13, 36
Asase Efua/Yaa, 28
Asona, 30-31
Asuansi Farm Institute, 30
Asymmetry, 71, 145
Atseow, 135
Augustine, St., 91
Authoritarianism, 117
Authority, 65, 92, 146

Autonomy, 113, 147
Awareness, 8, 54, 84, 146-147
Awerekyekyer, 54-56
Awutu-Effutu-Senya, 6
Ayamhyehye, 55
Ayee-gu, 135
Ayeekoo, 122

Baawah, 30
Balance, 5, 12, 70, 72, 88, 113,
    126, 148
Baths, 44, 82
Beads, 47, 83, 87
Beautiful, 12, 21, 30, 35, 136-
    137
Bearer of destiny, 22
Beginning, 6-8, 27-28, 49, 67,
    75, 82, 84-85, 89, 97,
    108, 112, 116, 129-131,
    143-144, 147
Behavioral patterns, 54, 64
Belief, 3, 36-37, 40, 42, 59, 62,
    104, 118, 132, 148
Belonging, 33-34, 86
Beneficent mother, 32, 56
Blood meat, 74
Blood of the mother, 16, 20-
    21, 34, 74, 144
Blood relations, 33
Boat, 137
Bogya, 16, 22, 36
Boiled egg, 88-89
Bosom, 32, 60, 119, 127, 148
Boyhood training, 91
Breast-feeding, 67, 87
Burial, 9, 34, 46, 130-132, 135
Burial rites, 9, 130–135
Busia, K. A., 20, 25

Call-and-response, 122-123
Calvinism, 75
Catholic church, 38
Career goals, 102
Cause-and-effect, 93
Cessation of breath, 23
Chamber-pot, 88
Characteristic attributes, 40,
    49, 52, 60, 64
Cheating, 99
Childbirth, 36, 49, 52, 81
Childhood, 6, 8, 79, 81, 83,
    85, 87, 89, 92-93, 112,
    114
Christensen, James B., 16
Christian ministry, 52
Chukwukere, I., 17, 24
Citizenship, 144
Circumcision, 83
Citizen/s, 5, 8, 20, 50, 92, 118,
    139, 146
Civic duty, 11
Clairvoyance, 42, 62, 126, 145
Clergy, 41, 51-52, 55, 57, 73,
    83
Cloth diapers, 83, 87
Code of ethics, 113, 126
Coffin, 131-132, 137
Cognitive development, 6, 8,
    92-93, 100, 118
Collective infallibility
    solidarity, 36
    spirits, 13-14, 50-51, 60,
    63, 81, 140, 145
    truth, 58, 66, 99, 125,
    127, 148
    body, 12-17, 19, 21, 23-
    24, 31, 34-37, 39, 41,
    44, 51-52, 57, 73, 76,
    82, 84, 93, 111, 115,

120, 127, 130-131, 134
Community of faith, 4, 65-66
Compassion, 55-56, 64
Components, 19-24, 63
Communal responsibility, 104
Concoction, 44, 46
Conduit of spirit, 45
Consanguineous linear group, 33
Consciousness, 8, 32, 145
Contempt, 123-124, 148
Constellation, 29, 32
Consensus, 124
Contraction, 45
Copulation, 21, 144
Corpse, 9, 34, 39, 55, 103,
    115, 130-132, 134, 136,
    138-139
Cosmetic rite, 95
Cosmogony, 18, 28
Cosmology, 8
Council/of elders, 120
Counsellors, 126, 148
Crawling, 89
Creation myth, 37, 69, 124
Creative process, 21
Created order, 140
Creator, 104, 143
Creation story, 29-31
Crescent moon, 21, 32-33
Creation account, 29, 31, 37
Critical reflection, 7, 118, 147
Crocodiles, 109
Crow, 30
Cry, 3, 45, 66, 85-86, 89, 115
Cup, 66, 101, 122
Customary law, 123
Cut/s, 46, 53, 74, 148
Cyclical sudden infant deaths,
    39